THE H

Ethnography

Over the course of twenty-five years, Tom O'Neill has travelled frequently to Kathmandu and the Helambu region of Nepal to conduct fieldwork with the local Yolmo business owners and carpet weavers. *The Heart of Helambu* is an evocative account of his experiences in Nepal during a time of political and economic upheaval.

In his autoethnographic memoir, O'Neill reflects on the complex relationships he developed with his research participants: the carpet weavers, their families, and others in the communities which he studied. While exploring topics such as the export carpet industry, village politics and social reciprocity, child labour, human trafficking, and the role of the state, *The Heart of Helambu* offers a compelling account of ethnographic fieldwork's personal dimension and the ethical and emotional challenges that come with maintaining relationships across substantial social distances.

(Anthropological Horizons)

TOM O'NEILL is an associate professor in the Department of Child and Youth Studies at Brock University.

Anthropological Horizons

Editor: Michael Lambek, University of Toronto

This series, begun in 1991, focuses on theoretically informed ethnographic works addressing issues of mind and body, knowledge and power, equality and inequality, the individual and the collective. Interdisciplinary in its perspective, the series makes a unique contribution in several other academic disciplines: women's studies, history, philosophy, psychology, political science, and sociology.

For a list of the books published in this series see page 169.

TOM O'NEILL

The Heart of Helambu

Ethnography and Entanglement in Nepal

UNIVERSITY OF TORONTO PRESS
Toronto Buffalo London

© University of Toronto Press 2016
Toronto Buffalo London
www.utppublishing.com

ISBN 978-1-4875-0035-1 (cloth)
ISBN 978-1-4875-2023-6 (paper)

Library and Archives Canada Cataloguing in Publication

O'Neill, Tom, 1957–, author
The heart of Helambu : ethnography and entanglement in Nepal / Tom O'Neill.

(Anthropological horizons)
Includes bibliographical references and index.
ISBN 978-1-4875-0035-1 (cloth). – ISBN 978-1-4875-2023-6 (paper)

1. O'Neill, Tom, 1957 – Travel – Nepal – Helmu Region. 2. Ethnology – Fieldwork – Nepal – Helmu Region. 3. Helmu Region (Nepal) – Social life and customs. I. Title. II. Series: Anthropological horizons

GN635.N425O54   2016   305.80095496   C2016-900133-4

University of Toronto Press acknowledges the financial assistance to its publishing program of the Canada Council for the Arts and the Ontario Arts Council, an agency of the Government of Ontario.

Contents

List of Figures　vii

Acknowledgments　ix

1　Solidarity, in Little Pieces　3

2　They Kill Animals Only for the Gods　26

3　A Map of Boudhanath　46

4　You Should Not Be Too Big a Person　65

5　A Modest Chöten　84

6　Diverging Paths　102

7　A Family Problem　116

8　Narayanhiti　139

Selected Glossary of Nepali and Tibetan Terms　155

References　159

Index　165

Figures

2.1 Election banners on New Road, Kathmandu, April 1991   32
2.2 The voting queue at Yangrima, April 1991   41
3.1 The Boudhanath stupa, byrarung khashor, July 1994   48
3.2 Sketch map of Boudhanath, Ward 9, and the Jorpati VDC, October 1995   53
4.1 A graphic artist traces a carpet design, March 1995   68
4.2 Carpet weaver, Jorpati VDC, November 1998   72
5.1 Young men in Uttar Bhanjyang putting the final touches on a chöten, October 1998   86
5.2 Nechung's sign guiding trekkers to the "Heart of Helambu," October 1998   91
6.1 The completed chöten in Uttar Bhanjyang, October 1998   104
7.1 Communist Party student union demonstration outside the Indian Embassy, July 2003   120
8.1 Tourists outside the gates of the Narayanhiti Museum, May 2013   149

Acknowledgments

This book describes events that span a period of twenty-two years. My first trip to Nepal was sponsored by the non-government organization Canadian Crossroads International, which gave me an opportunity to work and study there. I am grateful to fellow "Crossroaders" Rob Stevens and Mary Gauld for their support and interest in my work in Nepal. Subsequent visits were made as part of my doctoral research at the McMaster University Department of Anthropology, postdoctoral research at the University of Western Ontario Department of Anthropology, and as a faculty member at the Brock University Department of Child and Youth Studies. Many of the students, faculty, and colleagues at those institutions have been important influences, but William Rodman, Matthew Cooper, Trudy Nicks, Richard Preston, Ann Herring, and Jean-Marc Philibert were particular sources of inspiration. Funding for this research was generously provided by the McMaster University Faculty of Graduate Studies, the Social Sciences and Humanities Research Council of Canada, and Brock University.

Previous iterations of this manuscript were presented to conferences of the American Association of Geographers, the American Anthropological Association, and the Canadian Anthropology Society. I am grateful to David Butz, Kathryn Besio, Lynne Milgram, and Andrew Causey for their feedback and assistance with those presentations. Several anonymous reviewers of this manuscript provided detailed, critical comments that challenged me to focus and refine this book into its present form. I thank them for the care they took with the manuscript.

Loris Gasparotto created the sketch map of Boudhanath and Jorpati, based on my original notes. All of the photographs are my own.

In Nepal the Tribhuvan University Department of Anthropology and the Centre for Nepal and Asian Studies assisted my work at several stages. Many other people in Nepal have been extremely helpful. All the characters in this book correspond to many of those people and, as I have used pseudonyms to protect their identity, I cannot name them here. I am most grateful for their assistance, trust, and friendship. I take full responsibility for my account of them in this book and hope that it will meet with their approval, for I have only affection for all of them. Some place names have similarly been changed to protect these identities. As I write, in July 2015, Nepal is recovering from a series of devastating earthquakes that compound immeasurably their tribulations, which I describe in this book. I am happy to say most of them are physically unharmed and are in the process of rebuilding their lives. Their resilience is inspiring, and I remain committed to continuing our friendship.

My wife, Tina Moffat, accompanied me through most of these experiences and offered a sympathetic ear and encouragement as I wrote this book, even while drawing my attention to the many typographic errors in the manuscript. This book is also a product of the love we shared in Kathmandu and thereafter.

A version of chapter five of this book, "A Modest Chöten" was previously published as "The Heart of Helambu" in the journal *Critical Arts: South-North Cultural and Media Studies* 26 (2), 2012, copyright © Critical Arts Projects & Unisa Press, reprinted by permission of Taylor & Francis Ltd, www.tandfonline.com, on behalf of Critical Arts Projects & Unisa Press.

It is a thorny undertaking, and more so than it seems, to follow a movement so wandering as that of our mind, to penetrate the opaque depths of its innermost folds, to pick out and immobilize the innumerable flutterings that agitate it. And, it is an extraordinary amusement which withdraws from the ordinary occupations of the world, yes, even from those most recommended. It is many years now that I have had only myself as object of my thoughts, and that I have been examining and studying only myself, and if I study anything else, it is in order to promptly apply it to myself, or rather within myself. And it does not seem to me that I am making a mistake if – as is done in the other sciences, which are incomparably less useful – I impart what is learned in this one, though I am hardly satisfied with the progress I have made. There is no description equal in difficulty, or certainly in usefulness, to the description of oneself.

Montaigne, "Of Practice," in *The Complete Essays* (1965)

THE HEART OF HELAMBU

Ethnography and Entanglement in Nepal

Chapter One

Solidarity, in Little Pieces

"You will forget about me after you return to Canada," Dorje Lama said sadly as I forced the zipper shut on a large canvas bag on the floor.

We were leaving Kathmandu in a few days, and I needed to pack the weight of my fieldwork as carefully as possible; over 100 kilograms of field notes, interview transcripts, survey results, books, clothes, and other pieces of a puzzle that needed to be fitted precisely into the straining bag. Searching for a polite way to dismiss Dorje so that I could carry on with my work, I replied, "I can never forget you; it is not possible."

Dorje eyed a deep red woollen carpet on the floor, folded and bound with thick twine. "I am sorry that I did not make you a carpet," he rued, "I have been very busy ..." He trailed off. I knew that he had been preoccupied during the past few months, having moved his carpet factory three times in order to be closer to running water, shadowing carpet showrooms in hopes of work, travelling to his village to hire weavers, and performing *puja* (daily devotion). He had vaguely offered to make me a carpet a few months earlier, a promise that I had forgotten until this moment. I reassured him that I was not expecting one and invited him to join us at the airport in the morning, as a number of our friends were meeting to see us off. He told me that he would try, and then he shuffled wistfully downstairs.

Leaving Kathmandu behind after fifteen months and returning to a world in which the need for water was hardly a concern would be a difficult transition. Soon I would be back in Canada, sifting through mountains of notes and transcripts as the memory of the faces and friendships that haunt all that verbiage fades. I would forget. I would say my farewells, depart, and likely never again see Dorje or most of the people I had come to know over the past year. I tried to defer the effect of this prediction by reorganizing the bag I had just packed, but no matter which way I did this, it would still be a formidable burden.

The next morning I felt a strange combination of emotions as I helped a reluctant taxi driver hoist two such bags, one belonging to me and the other to my wife, to the top of his aging and battered Toyota. I wanted to return to my home in sight of the shining water of Lake Ontario, but I also regretted having to leave behind my morning walk to the Boudhanath *stupa* (shrine), with its half-closed eyes overlooking the circumambulations of pilgrims and tourists. It was late October, and the pungent scent of butter lamps mingled with the crisp autumn air. This was a lull between the frenzied celebrations of Dasain and Tihar, and I wondered if I would ever see the festival of lights again. Our bags, though tightly fixed to the roof racks of the Toyota with rope, tilted dangerously from side to side as we crashed through the muddy potholes of the Ring Road on our way to the airport.

Our friend Kalsang Sherpa was waiting for us with of three of his employees, who heaved the bags into the customs inspection area as the taxi driver supervised, pocketed his fare, and disappeared back down the hill and into the smoky valley. Kalsang placed *khata* (silk scarves) around our shoulders and led us in to where the two bags were thrown onto an aluminum inspection table. The bored-looking man on the other side of the table seemed to light up as the bag appeared. He looked sharply at the weigh scale as the needle bounced hard at the furthest extent of its arc before settling well beyond the 100-kilogram mark. A sign taped to the scale warned that the maximum weight per bag was 25 kilos. Clearly there was a problem. One of the inspectors motioned for us to open our bags and, as their contents exploded onto the table, I produced my passport and presented my student visa. The men shook their heads. Kalsang explained that we were anthropologists who had lived for over a year in Boudhanath, and that the bags contained important documents that were important for our research. Still heads shook; the distinction between tourist and researcher was not relevant to His Majesty's customs officials. One of the men lectured us through the smoke of his cigarette: aircraft must be light to lift up past the hills that encircled the Kathmandu Valley, and excess weight was to be assessed at $10 US per kilo.

Kalsang placed his hands together in supplication and reached for a roll of money in the breast pocket of his shirt. His employees abandoned a jovial conversation and gathered behind him. Kalsang's hand paused at his pocket, fingering the money inside, as the customs officials cried out in protest. Even though I found the pace of language and the tangle of accents impossible to follow, I knew that the heated exchange between the men was not merely about power and indignation, it was a kind of performance, an almost ritualized clash of masculinities. Voices were raised, but there were still traces of smiles on faces. The confrontation sputtered. After a moment of silence, one of the customs officials pointed to my wallet and asked, "How much is there?" I opened the wallet and displayed its contents, about $100 US in cash and a few hundred rupees. "We'll take that," he said, and tore two baggage claim tickets from a dispenser. I surrendered the cash with relief and repacked the bags before they were sealed and conveyed out of sight.

Chuckling, Kalsang led us to the airport lounge. "I saved you quite a bit of money," he said, and it was true. Kalsang was a shrewd negotiator and seemed equally adept at dealing with His Majesty's Government officials, German tourists for whom he organized treks to his native Khumbu region, or market vendors who haggled over a better price for onions in the local bazaar. The customs officials could have made our departure most unpleasant, and I was grateful that Kalsang was there to ease our passage.

Once inside the lounge, we were met by a large coterie of friends, people whom we had lived and worked with over the past year: Shyam, our language teacher and research assistant, along with his family; Paljor Lama, school headmaster and itinerant entrepreneur; Narendra Poudel, *saahuji* (proprietor of a carpet factory), petty capitalist, poet, and research collaborator; a monk I knew only as Tashi, who somehow had befriended us in Boudhanath and was a regular guest for tea and conversation. Sitting at the end of the table was Nechung Lama, carpet master and teacher. To him I owed most of what I knew about the day-to-day operations of a carpet factory. Kalsang moved to the other end of the table and presided as both Tina, my wife, and I were adorned with ceremonial khatas and flower garlands, the parallel honours given by Nepal's Buddhists and Hindus, respectively. Tea arrived, on Kalsang's order, and we spent our remaining time among friends. With each of them I felt a particular bond and perhaps an obligation not to let this moment of solidarity fade with time, but I also knew that we were the centre of this community. We were the reason it existed at all.

We chatted, reminisced, plotted future projects, and listened as the children, enjoying a day away from school, attempted puns and riddles in English. All the while, I kept a keen eye on the door, looking for Dorje Lama, the one character who was absent from the scene. He never appeared, and I would never see him again on any of my subsequent trips to Kathmandu. Finally, our boarding call was made. Kalsang stage-managed a group photograph on the observation platform outside, under a sign that read, "Welcome to Tribhuvan International Airport." Everyone posed, pictures were taken, and the community dispersed after a final farewell.

International airports are liminal spaces. Past each threshold, an aspect of one's individual status is stripped away as one enters a labyrinth that connects the local to the world beyond. Once past passport control, our visas were cancelled, so there could be no going back to the way things were. Through the gates of metal detectors, boarding passes initialled, we entered the sterile waiting area to wait or browse the duty-free shops with shelves lined with Canadian whisky, French liqueurs, and Swiss chocolates. There was a distinct smell of Camel cigarettes and air conditioning. Our boarding passes were then separated, leaving us with only a stub to enter the labyrinth's centre, an aging Royal Nepal Airlines 707, where we are between states, between times, between selves. An airline official ordered us to place the khata and garlands, still draped over our shoulders, into a garbage can that stood alone in the corridor leading to the plane.

The single airstrip grew smaller and disappeared. This moment marks a personal transition from the field and fieldwork to home and homework, and it is a moment that will never be repeated. After 1995 the changing interior of the airport reflected Nepal's darkening mood, and political instability and insurgency turned its internal thresholds into lines of battle. After the hijacking of an Air India flight from Kathmandu in 1999, all non-passengers were barred from the terminal building, and the lounge and observation deck were closed to all. The welcome sign is still there, as far as I know, but no one but airport staff can see it. By 2003 the liminal zone of exclusion was expanded as soldiers touting Belgian-made semi-automatic weapons thoroughly checked all documents at a checkpoint outside the terminal building before waving people through razor-wire barriers to the terminal building. Nepalese friends were no longer welcome, and were treated as potential terrorists or revolutionaries.

People have always been moved, physically, culturally, and personally by historical forces that are predictable only in hindsight.

Nepal's sorry decline since 1995 has sent many of my Nepalese friends into strange territory, territory marked by suffering and resignation. Several of the people in that final photograph are now dead, while others have been chased from their homes by insurgents or have lost their livelihoods, owing to an economy that collapsed during much of that time. In 1996 Dorje Lama could no longer sustainably produce cheap carpets for the European market, so he closed shop and went to live in a cave. For three years, three months, and three days he lived alone, seeking vision, purification, and transformation through immobility, sitting in daily meditation. The self-discipline of his meditation retreat seems a formidable task, and I often speculate that it was a traditional response to a contemporary failure, a way of reconciling not only lost wealth, but also a loss of secular status. I can never know for certain because I lost track of him afterwards and so could never ask him about his retreat. We both moved to new places, seeking stability and progress, careers and enlightenment, or, for Dorje, even just running water.

People from Dorje's village often refer to the rest of the world as that which is "below" them, in a topographic and perhaps even a moral sense. His region, Helambu, sits in the foothills of the Langtang Himalaya, and is a Buddhist redoubt in what was then an officially Hindu kingdom. My return to a foreign home, down in the developed world, marked the threshold between ethnographic fieldwork and a period of reflection, analysis and writing. "Fieldwork" is, however, an archaic metaphor for what anthropologists do because it is spatial, not temporal, fixed, not dynamic, pastoral, not cosmopolitan. I have been conducting fieldwork in Nepal since 1991, first as an undergraduate anthropology student doing volunteer work, then as a graduate student working on a PhD dissertation, later for postdoctoral work, and now as a faculty member at a small Ontario university. Throughout that time I have worked with the same people and in the same places in Nepal and observed the changes during this volatile period in Nepal's history: the general elections of 1991 and 1994 that introduced modern multiparty democracy; the increasing demand for human and, in particular, children's rights; the rise and decline of the carpet industry in Kathmandu in which fortunes were made and squandered; the transnational flight from economic and political decline; and a civil conflict that threatened to destroy whatever meagre gains were made in the past decade.

I observe these changes from a distance; writing about them has been a key ingredient in my own modest professional contribution, my accumulation of cultural and material capital. Anthropologists and other scholars in cosmopolitan centres often make their mark by peddling the problems of others, or of the "Other" for that matter, into lucrative academic careers. Countless monographs, articles, and research reports document the predations of global capitalism, social militarization, inequality, and the injustice that many of the people I came to know in Nepal were compelled to respond to at a much more intimate level. History affects them directly in ways that I can only helplessly observe. What I hope to accomplish with this book is an account of that decade that keeps this dialectic constantly present, by reopening my field notes and memories in the light of what we now know, as well as in the light of my continuing effort to maintain solidarity with the people who still speak to me in those notes.

The notes that I packed away that day as Dorje Lama reflected on our extinguished acquaintance have been transcribed, coded, annotated, and read over until almost committed to memory or, rather, until they have been joined to other recollections that are not so concretely documented. In addition to the formal interview recordings and survey data organized, "cleaned," and uploaded to a computer database, there are research field notes, observational data, and theoretical speculations in diary form. Included are personal diaries in which are recorded dreams; tangential debates on politics, religion, and sexuality; and short reviews of novels and films. There are several scratch books containing scribbled notes, drafts of forms, papers, diagrams of conceptual frameworks, lists of Nepali words and terms, and doodles penned out of sheer boredom. In one such book there is evidence of my attempts to write my name in Nepali, under instruction from a hotel desk clerk; this remains the only thing I can write in Devanagri script. In yet another book is my sketch of a dissertation I never wrote, having had to modify my plans to accommodate the theoretical obsessions of the day, to advance common knowledge, and contribute to disciplinary dialogue.

These are private documents, the documents that most anthropologists commit to cardboard boxes that fill filing cabinets, closets, and attics. Most of these notes are for our eyes only: we retrieve and use them in our work only when it can be demonstrated that they support our analysis and are subordinated to the higher aims of ethnographic writing. Otherwise they are too personal, irrelevant, or even boring for our readers and our colleagues, who are trained to interrogate the authority of our claims. This is a particularly violent form of self-censorship that erases accounts of the personal, the biographical, and the conversational nature of ethnographic fieldwork. It is a literary strategy of eliminating the author from the work and constructing an illusion of objective authority. Most anthropologists are well aware of these issues, particularly since the watershed publication of *Writing Culture* (Clifford and Marcus, 1986), which brought a postmodern sensibility and a revived interest in narrativity to the work of ethnography. Yet the lessons of that book were never broadly accepted, as most anthropologists are reluctant to completely expose themselves and what they do to the scrutiny of their peers. Objective ethnographic authority continues to dominate our writing, and, for the most part, those personal experiences remain in their boxes, regardless of the formative role they may have played in how anthropologists constructed, or rather co-constructed, their ethnographies.

* * *

In the fieldwork stories that follow, I try to restore the personal as a focal point, adding to Michael Jackson's (1998, 33) observation that "to reclaim narrative is to retrace history to a time when direct experience constituted a form of truth, when wisdom and knowledge had not parted company." To tell a story about fieldwork is to re-experience the process of entanglement with others, a process that is intersubjective, but that we experience individually. Through fieldwork we enter into others' lives: we are invited into their homes to hear their stories; share intimate details of their days; accept their food, their gifts, and their affection. Banishing the personal from our ethnographic narratives elides the many encounters, negotiations, cultural miscues, and personal commitments that provide the foundation for our ethnographic stories.

I often think of Dorje Lama alone in his cave, cloistered from all human contact save for the volunteers who passed supplies through his doorway. No speaking, silence but for the chanting, pungent smoke rising from butter lamps and incense. No conversation, only inward vision-seeking and summoning of spiritual powers from the darkness and from his own imagination, prefigured by a rich visual tradition of Tibetan art and literature. The lengthy meditation he undertook is the most rigorous form of voluntary isolation that I know – an act of world denial that must have been considerable for a young man like Dorje: a family man, a popular man, a man in his own world. It is an act that I find both puzzling and admirable; for where others would escape failure with flight, alcohol, or merely submission, Dorje called upon his own traditional resources to achieve redemption. In a context that emphasizes public religious performance and a culture that subordinates self-interest to the needs of the family and the village, Dorje's choice was one of the few options where one could privately pursue such redemption.

However, this is my story, based as it is on my encounters with Dorje and his family on numerous occasions, a tale corroborated by my notes on other fieldwork encounters and organized along narrative lines that were founded on my personal experience. There are other stories, of course, but I cannot tell those stories. I cannot even, accurately, relate Dorje's story, not only because I have never been able to meet with him again, but also because I am not sure that he could articulate that story in a language that would fully account for his inward experience and motivation. The product of ethnography, the story told, does not have a life of its own outside that of its teller. This is to say not that the people in that narrative, the places and cultures in which they live, are figments of our imagination, but only that they do not speak through those stories in a voice that is unmediated by our own. Geertz (1988, 145) coined the term "ethnographic ventriloquism" to describe the absurd claim that the ethnographer's voice and the voice of the Other are one and the same, that we are speaking not only for the Other, but authentically *as* the Other. Geertz's ventriloquists seem to be unaware that they are throwing their voices. That is the awareness I am trying to animate here. Our own biographies, I suggest, play a critical role in our redescriptions of others, but, as in Dorje's cave meditations, our explorations begin with who we are, and who we are is not fixed; we are constantly evolving into someone else. Like the flame in Dorje's butter lamp, we consume new experience as oxygen, and who we are is reflected and refracted from outside ourselves, glimmering in the darkness. In our understanding of Others, not only do we hear them, but we are also transformed in the listening.

Dennis Tedlock (1983, 324) argues for the "betweeness of the world" of anthropological dialogue instead of an analogical tradition that, he observed, "literally means 'talking above,' 'talking beyond,' or 'talking later,'" which dominates the discourse of social anthropology even now. I prefer to think of my conversation with Dorje in this light, as a conversation with a real person who has a theory, more or less, about why we are talking and what it is that we are talking about. Dorje, moreover, has a theory about me, and people like me. It is a theory that he shares, debates, and modifies as he converses with me and many others.

These theories are also a part of the text, also subject to translation and analysis, and also part of the story that ethnographers must tell about the texts and experiences they collect. If the aim of analogical ethnography is to provide a univocal, authoritative, and rational account of a culture or global cultural processes, then I see this narrative as one that reflexively recognizes the dialogue, the in-betweenness, of ethnography.

The Heart of Helambu is inspired by recent trends in autoethnography in which, according to Norman Denzin (2006), research interests intersect with the researcher's personal life. The term "autoethnography" first enters our lexicon, as far as I can tell, in a 1975 article by Karl Heider (1975, 3) about how the Dani of Irian Jaya understood their own world, that is, how they narrated themselves as a people in response to the question, simply put, "what do people do?" For Heider, the "auto" of "autoethnography" is derived from "autochthonous," the native point of view that emphasized routine subsistence activities rather than the ceremonial and conflict activities that dominated outsider accounts of Dani culture. Following Tedlock, however, the native point of view should be understood as but one side of a dialogue, though a dialogue that involves super and subordinate speakers. Mary Louise Pratt, in her book *Imperial Eyes* (1992, 7), elaborates on the idea of autoethnography through post-colonial theory: "auto-ethnography involves a partial collaboration with and appropriation of the idioms of the conqueror." In these early articulations of the term, "autoethnography" is something that others – the subordinated, colonized, and marginalized – do. Central to Pratt's view is the notion that the conversations are carried out between unequal speakers, and the language of the dominant overpowers that of the dominated; they respond to our categories, which we construct for our oppressive purposes.

A more common usage of autoethnography reverses this dynamic. It is the researcher who autoethnographs, not the "subordinates" who are subjects of the research. In this second view, autoethnography is a reflexive technique that positions the researcher as a central figure in an ethnographic account (see, e.g., Denzin 2003; Ellis 2004). This may be so in order to explicate the relations of power inherent in field relationships, or it may be so in order to position the researcher herself as both a researcher and a research subject, reflecting the "postmodernist" critique of objectivity and the view of individual identity as contingent, malleable, and ever changing (Reed-Danahay 1997). The "auto" of autoethnography in this case comes from "autobiography."

Autoethnography has been advocated as a legitimate qualitative research technique that is to be distinguished from autobiography through its attention to the inward gaze at the self, identity, and personal meaning, and to the outward gaze of standard ethnography at the life worlds of cultural "others."

Though both of these understandings of autoethnography appear to be distinct, both describe techniques of communicating across cultural boundaries. Pratt's emphasis on colonial domination arose out of her work on nineteenth-century travel writing, while contemporary autoethnography deals with many diverse fields in which the front lines of power are not nearly as clear. As a literary genre, autoethnography has provided space for the merging of autobiography and ethnography in accounts of personal transformation that challenge the assumptions in classical ethnography. Not unsurprisingly, it is a genre that is still regarded with some suspicion, if not outright derision, among professional ethnographers. George Marcus (1998, 585), in a review of Deborah Reed-Danahay's *Auto/ethnography: Rewriting the Self and the Social* (1997), argues that the attention autoethnographers pay to the particular is both a virtue and a limitation, yielding accounts that are "rich in setting" yet "[relieve] ... the inclination or responsibility to develop implication." Scholarship and analysis, on the one hand, evocation and reflection on the other – and only if it serves our responsibility as social scientists to explain what we observe.

Autoethnography can be something that ethnographers, trained in the art of developing implication, use to "strategically alter the way an audience of dominant outsiders understands the subordinate group," as David Butz and Kathryn Besio (2004, 353) put it, and thus challenge the political and epistemological position from which knowledge about the Other is generated. A few ethnographers, however, choose to write without overtly developing implication by conventional means. Writers such as Ruth Behar in *The Vulnerable Observer: Anthropology That Breaks Your Heart* (1996) and Paul Stoller in *Stranger in the Valley of the Sick* (2004) have written highly personal ethnographies that evoke their own transformation in the field or after their return from it. For Behar and Stoller it is the subordinate Other who becomes the teacher, the inspiration to change. Behar, in particular, explores the dynamics of fieldwork on personal ontology: "Do you learn anything about Spaniards, Mexicans, Jews, Cubans, Jubans, from reading these essays?" And I imagine myself replying, "Only insofar as you are willing to view them from the perspective of an anthropologist who has come to know others by knowing herself, and know herself by knowing others" (1997, 33).

Evocation and personal reflection are hardly the stuff of most professional ethnography. Indeed, most of the social sciences have quite forgotten that the self is the starting point for all knowing. In Ronald Pelias's *A Methodology of the Heart: Evoking Academic and Daily Life* (2004), the concept of self as starting point becomes the focus of the autoethnographic gaze. Pelias, who is not an anthropologist or a fieldworking social scientist and, as such, is therefore free to experiment with ethnographic conventions much more readily, evokes this starting point as "the academic tourist," an observer observing himself engaged in the everyday mundane academic practices that circumscribe the underlying privilege of the scholar. As the ethnographic gaze is directed to the Other, the autoethnographic gaze is directed to the self as though the self were Other.

Pelias's narrative of academic life intentionally leaves the "development of implication" to the reader – a literary strategy, but hardly an ethnographic one. For some, to eschew analysis and theory is to leave undone a central task of ethnographic writing. For others, it is better to retreat to the purely fictional realm of literature. Camilla Gibb, a Canadian anthropologist who defected entirely to literature, describes in her essay "An Anthropologist Undone" the intense personal struggle that she faced while doing fieldwork in East Africa, where the person "that lives with her boyfriend in England, struggles with sanity, drinks too many pints at the pub, wears short skirts and steel-toed boots" had to be concealed behind the veil in the conservative Islamic community she studied (2005a, 218). After her return from the field, she struggled again with her alienation from her former life at Oxford University and from the academic path that she had set out on, eventually concluding that "fiction might be the language of the anthropologist unbound from the narrative conventions of the discipline, the conventions of critique, the contextual and theoretical positioning which more often appear to obfuscate and alienate than they do to illuminate and include" (225).

Alienation is a starting point for fieldwork. Unlike tourists, fieldworkers attempt to move beyond their personal predispositions, their *habitus*, to participate in the predispositions of the Other. For all of the varied reasons that people choose to become anthropologists and write ethnographies, one commonality may be that they are willing to attempt that movement. Pierre Bourdieu describes this act of self-alienation as a "spiritual exercise" or self-transcendence that displaces our commonplace sense of Others, and as an "intellectual love" of a "supreme form of knowledge" (1999, 614). Bourdieu's metaphysic dominates the professional ethos of anthropology, an ethos that continues to privilege the analytic over the evocative. Gibb's preference, and my own, is for an erotic love that is a love of connection and experience, in contrast to Bourdieu's *kairos* of pure science. It is the faith in the latter that continues to influence objectivist ethnography and a desire for the former that leads some of us to write autoethnographies in which we explore the dynamic of self-alienation and transcendence in our fieldwork and in life afterwards.

Unlike Camilla Gibb, however, I do not think that it is necessary to abandon ethnography in order to do this or, at least, that this dynamic of alienation and transcendence is best used as the raw material for ethnographically informed works of fiction such as *Sweetness in the Belly* (Gibb 2005b). While writing fiction frees imagination and voice from the constraints of "developing implication," there is also potential for documentary autoethnography to fuse evocation and analysis while avoiding the perils of overt solipsism and theoretical objectification. This is what I am attempting here, knowing and expecting that the result may not satisfy readers looking for a conventional ethnography that pursues an explicit methodological and theoretical agenda.

Writing about fieldwork entanglements forces the writer to question the nature of self and Other, revealing ironies of claiming to know either. Paul Stoller (2007) suggests that there is a tension between losing and keeping control of our narratives when we write reflectively, and he points out that, for the most part, our own stories may be interesting only to ourselves. The danger of disappearing into the chaotic details of personal fieldwork experience and failing to provide a patterned interpretation for our readers looms large, but if our narratives are told from an objective, and objectifying, distance, then we are failing to acknowledge the dialogical nature of what we do.

Fieldwork is a purposeful behaviour, the work of which is knowing how to organize and record our experience so that at least some ordered semblance of it can be woven into a dissertation or monograph. Our mapping, measuring, recording, and inscribing must appear to be carefully premeditated and scripted, for, as Bourdieu (1998, 3) states, "the researcher, both more modest and more ambitious than the collector of curiosities, seeks to apprehend the structures and mechanisms that are overlooked – though for different reasons – by the native and the foreigner alike." This formidable responsibility of seeing beyond familiarity and through exoticism is one that I have accepted, apparently, as an anthropologist. For Bourdieu, such vision is a requirement for revealing a "universally valid" model of the underlying structure of social space. As for me, this aim is one that I have inherited with a profession that I have wandered into, but unlike Bourdieu, a scholar I have always admired and tried at times to emulate, my faith in the revelatory power of rational inquiry is in something of a crisis.

Ambition fuels most scholarship. It feeds the growth of disciplines, universities, research institutes, and celebrity careers. Bourdieu's faith that scholarship leads to self-transcendence, a coming to know more than one is, to see beyond appearances and penetrate to the inner workings of social space is shared by most researchers. Modesty lies in surrendering our scholarly self to a loftier ambition, of ignoring basic cravings to feed this vision of the invisible. Scholarly ambition is in tension with the modesty that makes it possible in the first place.

What is left of fieldwork, after it is done, are our notes, photographs, and memories. All three distort in their own manner, yet they are the material from which ethnography is constructed. Jens Qvortrup (2008) observed that research is about losing information in an organized fashion, stripping away the extraneous to reveal the bare outlines of analytic narrative. One of the first pieces to go is the sense that the fieldwork is a personal encounter with others. Tedlock (1983, 331) calls this "the tactical avoidance of full and open dialogue" that characterizes analogical ethnography. Ethnographies, after all, must relate a cohesive pattern of explanation, and attention to idiosyncrasy and contingency obscures the vision.

I have only two transcribed interviews, one survey data sheet, and ten observation sheets to account for, empirically, my contact with Dorje Lama, which can be augmented with my field notes and several photographs. Dorje's interviews are painfully brief, partly because of my limited ability in spoken Nepali at the time they were conducted. I had been taught formal conversational Nepali for several months before beginning my research, but I often struggled to understand and be understood in the local Nepali dialect that Dorje and other carpet makers in Boudhanath used. Nepali was, moreover, a second language for both of us, as in his own home Dorje spoke in the Tibetan dialect of Helambu, which is a language I remain unfamiliar with. Dorje's reticence, however, was also because he was, as they say, a man of few words. Trying to articulate responses to things that perhaps he had not thought about or formulated into words before was something of a chore for him. I gradually came to the realization that I would learn far more from Dorje by sipping tea with him in his living room than by forcing him to speak in a prescribed fashion into a microphone. Most of the interviews were translated with the assistance of my assistant, Shyam, and as my ability with the language has grown over the years I have come to recognize the imperfect glosses and interpretations they contained. Nevertheless, the interviews are the most concrete remnant of our time together, and occasionally I dig out the original recordings to hear them in Nepali. Listening to them often reveals how translations committed to paper are often inadequate.

According to Walter Benjamin (1968, 78), good translations "must lovingly and in detail incorporate the original's mode of signification, thus making both the original and the translation recognizable as fragments of a greater language." An analytic approach would have me attempt to untangle the "modes of signification" that are unique to his culture from all of the other forms of inauthentic and idiosyncratic babble that his text contains. Kirsten Hastrup (1997, 352) states that anthropology today is no longer the study of "semantic spaces accounting for the meaning of individual action and speech ... it is a theorization of the contact zone," that is, the investigation of discrete cultural traits no longer makes sense (if it ever really did) in a time in which global contact between peoples shapes all semantic space. But the task of discriminating between semantic spaces seems to remain central to what we do, as does the notion that there are objective forces that shape them. When Marx and Engels (1967, 14) famously declared that the "phantoms formed in the human brain are also, necessarily, sublimates of their material life forces," he was proposing one of many versions of these forces. While Bourdieu disagreed with the substance of Marx's analytical starting point of "men in the flesh," he shared the view that analysis is possible because there is a "universal validity" in how we organize social life, be it the logic of dialectical materialism or the geometry of social fields. In both cases there is an underlying structure that lies, invisible, behind appearances.

In both cases also epistemology is based on a metaphysic. The problem with analyses of "men in the flesh," or of the underlying structures that determine their world, is that outsider accounts of fleshy lives can be given only in the outsider's language. They cannot be true accounts. As Richard Rorty (1989, 5) points out, "to say that truth is not out there is simply to say that where there are no sentences, there is no truth, that sentences are elements of human languages, and that human languages are human creations." The discourse of academic anthropology, the universe to which I am most often obligated to communicate, is also present in our conversation, not only in the various probing techniques we use to organize the loss of information, but also in the nature of the questions asked. Ours is a comparative discipline and our conversation must be designed to resonate with other conversations carried out by other anthropologists in other contexts. The questions I put to Dorje were composed in Canada, not in Nepal, and were based on a reading of apposite ethnographic accounts. They needed to be approved by an institutional research ethics committee before we could speak, or rather, before I could record. In a sense, then, the conversation is not only between Dorje and me, but between multiple universes of discourse, something akin to what Mikhail Bakhtin (1981) called "heteroglossia": the babble of invisible participants in our conversation.

Dorje, moreover, has become an ethnographic character, here and elsewhere, who corresponds to a real person. That correspondence is constructed by me with an eye to remain true both to my notes and memories of our conversations, and to the demand that I make his character understandable in the ethnographic genre. At conferences, in research articles, and in book chapters, I struggle to make his character fit in a universe of scholarly discourse about petty capitalism, about child labour, children's rights, sex trafficking, transnationalism, and contested ethnic identity. In each of these spaces, Dorje has been sculpted to fit a conversation that he, if asked, might well have little interest in.

Ethnographic authority is most effectively achieved when the voice of the Other is heavily edited, sculpted, and reformed to conjure various kinds of revelation. It is more effective, still, when all evidence of the work of construction is hidden from view, so that this voice appears to speak its own story, when in effect what is heard is a kind of ethnographic ventriloquism. As I plumb Dorje's interview records for their truths, I am conscious that seemingly minor editorial decisions are mine alone, as he is not here with me to consult . I am also conscious of the immense violence that I am capable of committing on our conversation, as I force it into academic and theoretical conversations in which the goal is to penetrate to the reflexes behind his words. The work of analysis can betray the dialogue that it is based on.

In writing autoethnographically about fieldwork entanglements, I have had to set aside the pursuit of universally valid models and look for alternative visions of what ethnography could be. Rorty (1989, 94) suggests another possibility – evoking the fine-grained detail of the social in its specific forms:

> the disciplines which were once charged with penetrating behind the many private appearances to the one general reality – theology, science, philosophy – were the ones which were expected to bind human beings together, and thus to eliminate cruelty. Within an ironist culture, by contrast, it is the disciplines which specialize in thick description of the private and idiosyncratic which are assigned this job. In particular, novels and ethnographies which sensitize one to the pain of those who do not speak our language must do the job which the demonstrations of a common humanity were supposed to do. Solidarity has to be constructed out of little pieces, rather than found already waiting, in the form of an ur-language which all of us recognize when we hear it.

Rorty's project has been, by and large, to redeem empathy, as a basis of solidarity, from the wreckage of the enlightenment wrought by its collision with the postmodern critique. His casting of ethnography and the novel in the same family of genres is, on the surface, provocative. Ethnography is an empirical form based on real life, actual events, and the meticulous collection and analysis of data, whereas novels are the work of literary imagination. It might be argued that he has not read much ethnography, but clearly he has; his reading of ethnography is because of its ability to "sensitize one to the pain of those who do not speak our language," a task that I take as calling for narratives that are evocative, rich in character, and in the predicaments that life places these characters in. Lynn Hunt (2007) has recently argued that literature, specifically the novel, played an important cultural role in the emergence of human rights discourse because it not only allows, but depends upon, the empathic faculties of the reader. Rorty suggests that ethnography, like the novel, is at its best when it engages the ability of the reader to recognize the pain and the subjectivity of others. Action flows from empathy, not only, or not primarily, from analysis.

The analysis of fieldwork is useful for bringing to account the global forces that pit people against each other in cruel competition, but the intersubjective evocation of fieldwork experience may better evoke the kind of empathetic reading that allows us to recognize suffering, not only the suffering that arises from cruelty, but also the everyday sort that comes from just struggling to live. This empathy is what Dorje and

I built, piece by piece, through the practice of fieldwork. Our mutual entanglement is what constitutes our common humanity, and writing about it exposes the sometimes painful asymmetries between our lives as well as the struggles that are shared.

In this book, I focus on a formative series of collaborations that shaped my own ethnographic biography. These collaborations were, and remain, attempts at solidarity making if "solidarity" is taken to mean a mutual dependence that is emergent, fragile, and, as in most human relationships, inherently messy. At its heart are my collaborations with a specific group of carpet manufacturers and weavers from a small hamlet located in Helambu – Dorje Lama's village – about a day's walk northeast of Kathmandu. While most ethnographies redescribe specific, discrete research projects, this one spans a decade and recounts a series of ethnographic projects, along with the ongoing evolution of this solidarity making, and my ongoing entanglements in Nepal.

What do others think we are doing, travelling so far from home to do something that we call research? For Dorje, and indeed for most of the Nepalese men and women that I have worked with, there is little in language or experience that suggests a cognate activity. Research, they know, is something that foreigners do, as well a growing number of Nepalese scholars, working either for development NGOs or in universities. Some communities in Nepal, of course, are fully familiar with foreigners as researchers and do distinguish between them and other foreigners in Nepal for reasons such as tourism, development work, and commerce. Groups like the Sherpas of the Solu-Khumbu region, the Gurung of the midwest, and the Newars of the Kathmandu Valley have had ample ethnographic attention from both European and North American anthropologists. In the case of the Sherpas, this attention fills entire bookshelves in university libraries and has contributed to their recognition globally, iconically perhaps, as Himalayan mountain people: brave, strong, hospitable, and deeply committed to their Buddhist faith (Fisher, 1990; Adams 1996; Ortner 1989, 2001). Though some people from Dorje's home in the Helambu region also call themselves Sherpa, they bear only a distant relationship to the people of Solu-Khumbu, speak a different Tibetan dialect, and play a different historical role in their connections with the Nepalese state. While there is some fine literature on the people of Helambu, it has neither the volume nor the prestige of the literature on their more famous namesakes. Consequently, Dorje's people, who call themselves lamas, draw little capital worldwide from their ethnic identity. Many of them may have seen the occasional foreign trekker hiking down to Melamchi Pul from Gosainkund, but foreign tourism, development work, and research do not play the transformative role in Helambu that they do elsewhere.

The Helambu region stretches between two high ridges that tower over the Melamchi river in the foothills of the Langtang range, about 50 kilometres northeast of the Kathmandu Valley. It has frequently been described as the "Yolmo region" by many western scholars in reference to the people who inhabit these ridges. Dorje Lama is a *Yolmowa* (lit. person of Yolmo), a descendent of the original Tibetan settlers who inhabited this region over 300 years ago. He speaks a Tibetan dialect known as Yolmo and has learned to read Tibetan scriptures, as have most Yolmo men. This ability marks him as a "reading *lama*," something that distinguishes him and other Yolmowa from other Tibeto-Burman ethnic groups who inhabit the neighbouring hills and valleys. The Yolmo clans date back to the arrival of NgaCha Shakya Zangpo, a powerful Tibetan lama who helped to restore the sacred Buddhist stupa at Boudhanath before founding an influential *gonpa* (temple) in Helambu. Thus, the connection between the Yolmo gonpa of Helambu and the great Buddhist stupa at Boudhanath, now located in a bustling suburb of Kathmandu, is intimate and long-standing.

Yolmowa relationships with other hill peoples are extensive. Yolmo men served outlying Tamang as Buddhist lamas, performing religious puja for funerals and other life-cycle events. David Holmberg (1989), an anthropologist who has worked with Tamang communities, notes that the Tamang are nominally Buddhists as well, but that they lack the liturgical skills that Yolmo "reading lamas" can provide; in return, he argues, Tamang sacrificial priests provide ritual services that more orthodox Buddhists such as the Yolmo are reluctant to conduct because they involve killing animals that are considered to be sentient beings. The Tamang live in the hills surrounding the Yolmo region and even within it; in fact, they comprise the single largest ethnic group in the Sinhupalchok region that the Helambu area is part of. Those Tamang who live in close proximity to the Yolmo region share many cultural values with the Yolmo Buddhists and are economically tied to them as well. Nechung Lama, Dorje's friend and business associate, is Tamang, something that I did not learn until well into my work with them. However, the relationship between Tamang lama and Yolmo lama is not an equal one. The Tamang are designated in Nepal's traditional hierarchy of castes and ethnic groups (the *muluki ain*) as drinkers of alchohol and eaters of meat, both of which are prohibited for orthodox Hindus. The Yolmo too view the Tamang as their moral inferiors but, as fellow Buddhists, see them as subjects of their civilizing concern.

The Tibetan Buddhists that Shakya Lama is reputed to have established in Helambu settled the fertile ridges in villages centred around a network of temples that were built on lands granted to them by the Newar and, later, Shah kingdoms of the Kathmandu Valley. There has been a long-standing relationship between the Yolmo and the regimes that dominated them politically over time; more recently, Yolmo women served as servants, entertainers, and concubines to members of the ruling Rana family, which dominated all of Nepal until 1951. The land on which the Boudhanath stupa stands is held by the hereditary Chinya Lama, who originated from Melemchigaon, a Yolmo village located in northwest Helambu. In 1993, during my first fieldwork in Boudhanath, the then Chinya Lama was a controversial figure who had close political ties to the conservative Rastriya Prajantantra Party, which had its roots in the Rana family.

Despite this connection to Nepal's powerful elites, most Yolmo were farmers who grew barley, maize, and potatoes on terraces that swept down the steep ridges; others further up the valley were pastoralists, grazing herds of hybrid cattle in the high pastures. The lure of wages took many of the men to India and beyond to work as labourers on road wages; most recently, the carpet factories of the Kathmandu Valley and, later, lucrative menial work in the Persian Gulf or Southeast Asia beckoned Yolmo men and women to work, often remitting to families in Helambu. During my most recent visits I found many abandoned fields and villages inhabited mostly by elderly men and women throughout Helambu.

Robert Desjarlais, an American anthropologist who has had extensive experience with the Yolmo, notes an irony in recent Yolmo history: at a time when political freedom and autonomy for Nepal's ethnic minorities is growing, the threat of cultural disintegration looms large (2003, 11). Indeed, most elderly lamas that I spoke with expressed a similar concern, as their youth were moving away to Kathmandu and beyond, far from the gonpa-centred villages and hamlets that were, until recently, the secure location of Yolmo life and moral character.

This conservative conception of Yolmo culture is under threat from the exposure that many young lamas have with new cultural and economic influences far beyond their villages, but it is precisely this movement from the local to the global that interested me. One of the persistent challenges in my research was how or even if I could reconcile the relevance of the vast ethnographic vocabulary on the Helambu lamas with their contemporary role as urban entrepreneurs, labourers, consumers, and subjects of globalization. Concerns about culture loss must be teased from fears of culture change, fears that have become more acute in Nepal's recent rapid, uneven, and somewhat violent outward engagement with global political and economic influences. The many Yolmowa and Tamang that I met in Boudhanath, maintained both material and affective relationships with their home region and continued to practise their religious traditions. Some aspects of their culture, however, were in tension with the commodification and individualization of social relations that follow from global market logic.

The carpet industry, which I originally went to Nepal to study, was a development that allowed Yolmo and Tamang to directly participate in the global economy, offering some of them entrepreneurial opportunities to transcend the limited role in Nepal's economic and social life afforded to them by Nepal's Hindu elites. As the industry was founded by Tibetan refugees in the early 1960s and produced a uniquely Tibetan carpet, their Nepalese Yolmo and Tamang co-religionists were able to find opportunity by working first as weavers and then, as the industry grew, as autonomous subcontractors managing their own carpet production. In 1995 there were 233 informal sector operations in the Boudhanath area (including neighbouring Jorpati), 56 being operated by Tamangs and 32 by Yolmo subcontractors like Dorje (O'Neill, 2001). For a brief time until around 1995, the carpet industry experienced rapid growth and many young lamas, such as Dorje and Nechung, were able to raise their family income and settle into something like a middle-class urban lifestyle, but the informal nature of their production meant that they were the most vulnerable when markets shrank and Tibetan exporters stopped taking on subcontract orders. As the carpet market contracted after 1995, many of these Yolmo and Tamang subcontractors lost their livelihoods. Dorje lost his business and retreated to a cave; Nechung lost much more.

This is the suffering that this book refers to. It is not the traumatic suffering brought on by violent social upheavals (though many hundreds of thousands in Nepal were soon to experience them), but the everyday suffering of people trying to build their lives in rapidly shifting circumstances that rendered their efforts obsolete. My purpose in writing is to make some sense, affectively, of this suffering by finding my own place in it. It is not to sketch an analysis of the political and economic forces that conspired to alter Dorje and Nechung's lives so profoundly, to point fingers at international structures, and to assign blame for their fates. Dorje and Nechung may be authors of their own misfortune, just as I am the author of my own ethnographic entanglement with their fates.

Many anthropologists have observed that anthropology as a discipline emerged as a product of the colonial era (Asad 1991). Anthropologists were trained in elitist institutions and then sent to work in the peripheries of the imperial centres, where, in tandem with colonial agents, traders, and missionaries, they undertook the project of classifying and analysing subject peoples, constructing for each an orthodox ethnographic profile that defined their Otherness. Even though early on most anthropologists refused to collaborate with imperial projects of domination and assimilation, the discipline itself played a role in establishing an ethnomethodological taxonomy of cultural differences that continues to order our world. It is a methodology that can be seen at work in the halls of the Museum of Anthropology in Mexico City, in the records of the Human Resources Area Files, and, indeed, in the meetings of the American Anthropological Association. It claims, of course, to be no longer in the service of the imperial project. Anthropologists are at the cutting edge in the defence of aboriginal peoples around the world and in advocating for the working, subaltern, and deviant classes or subcultures that are threatened by the hegemony of global capital and Western cultural domination.

This advocacy was the spirit in which I approached Dorje and Nechung to participate in my project. I played the part of cosmopolitan scholar, interrogating their accounts of themselves for their multiple revelations. Dorje and Nechung were cast as the Other, worthy of my attention as an expert on the predicaments of traditional peoples undergoing rapid social change in a globalizing economy. Their position was as petty capitalist carpet producers floundering through the ebb and flow of global capital, at one juncture encouraging them to risk it all to succeed, at another pulling the rug, as it were, from under their feet (O'Neill 2005).

Many scholars write about globalization as the technological unfettering of markets and ideas to cross national and cultural boundaries as never before. Anthony Giddens (2003) has argued that globalization is a contradictory process. While it appears, on one hand, that globalization is imposing the hegemony of Western markets and ideas, he points out that it also underlies the growing cultural assertiveness of subaltern and indigenous peoples. This is, in part, because the global flow of capital, intellectual as well as material, provides new opportunities just as it closes down others. John and Jean Comaroff (2009) point out, for example, that many indigenous groups in Africa are abandoning traditional strategies of cultural assertion by shifting attention to the uses of intellectual property law and corporate organization to assert control over their own identity. This was also the case, initially, for Yolmo and Tamang carpet producers. One aspect of globalization, according to Arjun Appadurai (1998, 31), is that imagination has become a social practice that shapes the "negotiation between sites of agency (individuals) and globally defined fields of possibility."

However, the critics of globalization are not incorrect to condemn the growing inequality that the global flow of capital produces. The predicament that Dorje and Nechung found themselves in towards the end of my fieldwork speaks eloquently of how people can be lured by the enticing possibilities of globalization, only to be later dashed upon its rocks. One of globalization's most ardent critics, Zygmunt Bauman (1998, 4), states that transnational globals "set the tone and compose the rules of the life-game" that compel those fixed in the grip of global capitalism to experience a downward mobility marked by increasing inequality, forced cultural homogenization, and withering autonomy. By "globals," Bauman refers to those elites charged with overseeing capital flows: transnational executives, traders, specialists in international "development," and World Bank representatives. Few anthropologists would recognize themselves in that company.

I think it is fair to observe that Dorje, and likely most of the people I encountered while fieldworking, did see me and all other foreign anthropologists as "elite." Understandably so, as we all share one important characteristic with each other that they do not – we have the ability to travel, the leisure to study, and the affluence to consume. They perceive themselves as being fixed and struggling to adapt to modernizing changes being dictated from outside of the country. Some of these changes they embrace, some they reject, and others they fear. They see evidence of these changes all around them: rapid urbanization, precarious livelihood, hints of the good life, reminders of the bad; the palatial homes of Tibetan carpet magnates that they admire, aspire to, and to a degree covet; the frequent political strikes, campaigns, promises, and violence; the jets that roar into Tribhuvan airport over their rooftops on their way to London, Frankfurt, or Singapore.

What Dorje knew is that I would eventually get on one of the jets and fly home, leaving him to suffer those contradictions. Not only do we anthropologists study the contradictions of globalization, but we embody, and even thrive on, them. The day-to-day entanglements of doing fieldwork constantly reminded me of this fact. For however much people welcomed me into their lives, there were always reminders of my Otherness and the privilege disparity between our lives. We may suffer those contradictions too, but we rarely experience the consequences of them in the same life-or-death fashion that fieldwork participants do. We do not retreat into caves. We retreat into the academy: teaching anthropology courses, submitting grant applications, cobbling together the credentials to get tenure, and jetting around the world to deliver papers to conferences in exotic locales. We retreat into writing. We build careers and families while our notes, and indeed our memories, fade with time. We do not forget the people that we have worked with so much as replace them with versions of themselves that we are constantly revising, constantly inserting into professional discourse.

This book is meant to be about, and for, Dorje and Nechung and also about the many others who collaborated, knowingly or unknowingly, in my becoming an anthropologist. It begins in 1991, when I first travelled to Nepal and sought cross-cultural encounter, and then explores the different facets of fieldwork that represent the ongoing transformation of that initial encounter. It ends twenty-two years later with a description of a reunion with some of the central people and places of my field experience. Some of this book's images, anecdotes, and reflections are drawn from the weight of ethnographic diaries and notes that had been filed away, neglected, since my dissertation was completed, while others have been culled from hazy memory. These pieces are, in hindsight, difficult to circumscribe in words alone, as they have been revised so often in the interim that they resist restoration. I know more now than I did then, thanks in part to Dorje and his friends, as I have grown professionally and intellectually. The purpose of this book, however, is to remember that, beyond knowing more now than I knew then, who I am now has grown out of what I did then. It is in this dialectic that the ethnographer ceases to be an author who can be distinguished from his/her creation.

Chapter Two

They Kill Animals Only for the Gods

In 1991, after a short term as volunteer teacher at a school in the Khumbu Himalayas, I returned to Kathmandu resolved to learn more about Nepal and its culture. By late April, the Kathmandu Valley was hot and dusty, garbage collectors on strike left rotting piles of decaying matter on street corners everywhere, and people seemed edgy. Once in the city, any pretensions about my role as a teacher were quickly dispelled, as I immediately found myself at the immigration office having to renew my tourist visa for a fourth month. I was a tourist, no different from the throngs who huddled in the shade of pipal trees wearing tie-dyed tank tops, their hair in dreadlocks, their backpacks stuffed with incense and stale trail gorp. I tried hard not to look like them, but was fairly sure that this is how Nepalese officials saw me. In 1991 the maximum stay for tourists was nominally three months, but you could negotiate a fourth month if you could provide a plausible reason for staying on. In my pocket I had a scrap of paper with the name of a *tulku* (reincarnated lama) who lived in Boudhanath that had been passed to me by a tourist who had stayed briefly at Kalsang's lodge. On the visa renewal application I put down that I was studying *dharma* (religion) and that I needed the additional month to complete my studies.

    Having convinced the immigration officials of the validity of my extension request, I set out for Boudhanath to seek out Tulku Chokyi Nyima, a respected abbot and Buddhist *rinpoche* (teacher), who I had been told accepted Western students. Far from having to complete my studies with him, I wanted to get them started. I found his enormous monastery, pure white against the muddy fields that surrounded it. Entering its gates was to enter another world – well-tended gardens and clean-swept steps to the sanctuary clashed with a parking lot full of four-wheel-drive Toyota Pajeros. I eventually found the rinpoche inside the meditation hall. For a great lama, he looked fairly unremarkable, a pleasant, middle-aged Tibetan man who could have as easily been frying *momo* (dumpling) in the street as presiding over the transmission of a religious tradition. He greeted me warmly and genuinely, but as I spoke, I sensed that he was only partly listening. Finally, with a smile, he shook my hand and scuttled by to attend, he said, to his mother who was near death, but he agreed to meet with me when his work was done. He assigned some reading for me to do in the meantime – a biography of the Tibetan saint Milarepa (Lhalungpa 1979).

That book contains a paradigmatic account of how a student of dharma must be tested by the *guru* (master) for worthiness. One does not wander haphazardly into religious instruction as one would, say, register for an anthropology course without even knowing the origins of the discipline. In the book, Milarepa approaches the Tibetan guru Marpa for dharma instruction, but Marpa responds by instructing him to use his magical powers to bring a hailstorm upon some enemies and then to thwart an attack by mountain men on some of his followers. Milarepa uses his powers to accomplish these tasks, but Marpa is not satisfied. He instructs Milarepa to build a tower for his son. Before the tower is finished, Marpa returns and directs Milarepa to destroy it and rebuild it elsewhere in a different design. After Milarepa has completed the tower, Marpa orders him to destroy this one, too, claiming that he was drunk when he ordered its construction. When Milarepa questions Marpa's order to destroy yet a third tower, Marpa angrily challenges him to do his will or leave. Milarepa obediently does so and is rewarded with the teaching.

Having read the book, I returned to the monastery several times, but the lama was never there, or could not meet with me. After a couple of weeks of this routine, it looked as though my visa would expire without the benefit of his teachings. I mentioned my problem to one of the other Western students at the monastery, an American woman dressed in a traditional Tibetan dress who admonished my impatience, "Oh, he will test you." In the tradition of Milarepa and Marpa, initiates must be "tested," so that their worthiness for instruction can be assessed by the guru. I was suspicious, though, that a family death could be construed to present such a test and felt that this student, being one already found worthy, may have been embellishing the circumstances. Nevertheless, I persisted in trying to meet the rinpoche. After all, I had read the book that he had assigned and had many questions.

At about the same time as I was experimenting with Buddhist practice the anthropologist Peter Moran was conducting research with Westerners in search of dharma instruction from among Tibetan teachers in Boudhanath. These rinpoche offered seminars, meditation retreats, and ritual practices geared to Western audiences. According to Moran (2004), Western dharma students insisted on the importance of developing a close relationship with a rinpoche as crucial to spiritual advancement, as without a guru the elite knowledge of Vajrayana Buddhism (practised in most of these monasteries) would be impossible to obtain. Moran notes that the importance of the rinpoche is far less important to lay Tibetan Buddhists, who concern themselves less with elite religious knowledge and more with the practical application of dharma to daily life. Having already lived with lay Buddhists in the Khumbu, I was aware that the Buddhism imagined by many Western converts was vastly different the Buddhism practised by ordinary Buddhists in the Himalayas, but I persisted in my quest regardless. I finally managed to make an appointment for an audience in his apartment one morning. When I arrived, I was disappointed to find several other Westerners also waiting – a French woman bearing a bottle of brandy, her daughter, and a German man who ignored us as he pored over sheaves of Tibetan religious texts. I chatted amiably with the woman and her daughter, distracted by the Tibetan text that the man was reading. He could read Tibetan? I wanted to ask him what the text was about, but sensed that he would not have responded to my question. Finally, we were called into the rinpoche's apartment. The German man entered first, dropped to his knees, and prostrated himself before the rinpoche with his arms outstretched. The French woman and her daughter went next and gracefully sank to the floor, placing the bottle of brandy at the rinpoche's feet. I came next, but I was blocked by a powerful doubt. Their submissive gesture seemed alien to me. I had barely met this man and going through the motions of a prostration struck me as ridiculous. Embarrassed, I bowed my head, folded my hands together, and moved to sit with the small group at the guru's feet.

The rinpoche then spoke pleasantly to each of us, almost informally, in eloquent English. He thanked the French woman for the brandy, saying that he looked forward to trying it, and then distributed to each of us a small pinch of black powder from an embroidered silk pouch. Again I was at the threshold of the unfamiliar and watched as the other acolytes, obviously more familiar with these rituals than I, licked the powder eagerly from their palms. I licked up my mine and it tasted like cigarette ashes. The rinpoche and the German man began a detailed discussion of the text that he had brought with him as two young Nepalese men entered the room belatedly, prostrated, and joined the audience. The guru continued the textual exegesis, then, almost as a distraction, he greeted the two young men and offered them a pinch of black powder as well. As they licked it up, he turned to me and dropped another pinch into my hand. Confused, I took my second helping. He continued to chat with the Nepalese men, added a few comments to the German student, and stopped as if remembering something. He turned to me and asked: "You have already had some?" "Yes," I replied. "Well, I think you needed more. You have too much brain and not enough face." He smiled at me, impishly, turning back to the German man and his texts, leaving the remark intentionally cryptic. A puzzle for me to solve. It was not possible to be absolutely certain what he meant, but it appeared to be in regard to my unwillingness to prostrate myself as I entered, an incisive comment on my reluctance to stage an act of submission to a great teacher that is common in the Tibetan tradition. The others seemed to have little difficulty doing so, but perhaps they were not staging anything. Perhaps what they were performing was an authentic display of respect for their teacher. But given that my tourist visa was about to expire and it had taken several weeks to meet this man, to prostrate myself would have been decidedly inauthentic. Moreover, the fact that the other visitors had preceded me with their prostrations led me to act differently, to distinguish myself in some small way. Thus, this moment was one of a double alienation: one from my companions at the audience and the other from my moment with the guru.

Outside the monastery, deep ruts pressed into the mud by trucks were filled with rainwater. Children in blue uniforms leapt between them as bicycle-wallahs piloted their wares across. Above us the great stupa of Boudhanath towered over a ripening rice paddy and a cluster of red-brick tenements. I had failed my guru's test. Though I was to return and live nearby for over a year I never approached the rinpoche again. Yet the puzzle he presented me with that day remains. Too much brain, not enough face. Too much rationality, prejudgment, or complacency, perhaps, and not enough encounter or empathy. It is a dilemma that has marked my relationship with fieldwork and my own discipline ever since.

Tridevi Marg is one of the busiest streets in Kathmandu and an intersection of traditional power and modernity, where *tempo* (taxis) belching black smoke, hawkers peddling ersatz *gaine*-caste violins, knock-off Tiger Balm, and displays of unidentifiable "tribal" ornaments tumble into the streets in the shadow of the enormous red-brick Narayanhiti palace, the centre of the monarchy and political power since its construction in the 1960s. Directly across the street from the palace was the American Club, a high-security compound where, if admitted, one could obtain a beef hamburger in direct violation of the palace's Hindu laws. Outside, shadowy figures peddling hashish drifted by, avoiding eye contact, chanting "smoke ... smoke," as the soundtracks of bootleg American movies bellowed out of video cafes onto the narrow streets nearby. Beggars, with only rags covering their twisted bodies, stretched out their hands to the American, European, and Israeli tourists browsing shop windows or negotiating with taxi drivers.

On one corner of this contradictory scene, and divided from it by a rusting iron gate, lay the neglected gardens of the Keshar Mahal. Built in 1895 by Chandra Shumsher Rana, the autocratic ruler of the Kingdom of Gorkha, which dominated Nepal from 1846 to 1950, it is a decaying example of Rana opulence and now serves as an office for Nepal's Ministry of Education. A paved road winds from the street outside to its grand entrance, and one could imagine the landaus of state officials and foreign dignitaries rolling to a stop at the massive carved doors. Both Nepalese and European-style lion sculptures now guard the front entrance, signifying an earlier collaboration between the Gorkha and British empires. On the many occasions in which I was in Tridevi Marg, on compulsory visits to the adjacent immigration office, I escaped into the nostalgia of the Keshar Mahal.

Inside the ornate, crumbling façade of the mansion is the "Kaiser" library, as it is known, a window into Nepal's political past. Bookshelves there contain thousands of English-language books that date to the end of the Second World War, the complete works of Winston Churchill (whom Keshar Rana admired) and William Shakespeare, as well as ethnological texts by Spencer and Frazier. In a gallery on the second floor there were splendid portraits of members of the Rana clan in their imperial finery: Jung Bahadur Rana, the founder of the dynasty; Chandra Shumsher, the powerful leader who dominated Nepal in the early twentieth century; and Keshar himself, sporting a chest covered in military medals. There were photographs of hunting expeditions to the *tarai* region with the Prince of Wales, posing with his kill of now endangered Bengal tiger and one-horned rhinoceros. Signed portraits of Mohandas Gandhi and Emperor Hirohito hung amid metal bookcases containing books in Nepali and Sanskrit, and enormous wild buffalo trophy heads were mounted on the wall. The martial character of this detritus whispered of the ever present violence with which Nepal had been ruled for over a hundred years.

The contrast between the dusty reality claimed by the Keshar Mahal and events as they unfolded outside was striking. Keshar died in 1964, not long after the regime that ensured his hereditary privilege had fallen in 1950. He lived long enough to see the first chaotic democratic elections in 1960 and the royal coup of 1961 that imposed *panchayat* (partyless democracy) on the country, but he would scarcely have recognized the intense democratic energies of 1991. Beyond the Keshar Mahal's gates, thirty years later, Nepal was in the midst of new democratic elections and every available surface had been appropriated by political activists armed with cans of spray paint. In order to campaign to a still largely illiterate electorate, the election commission issued symbols to each party for campaigning purposes that were painted onto almost every available surface. The Nepal Congress Party, for example, was represented by a tree and the Rastriya Prajantantra Party (National Democratic Party) by the plough, an ironic symbol for a party made up largely of landowners. Many of the cows that freely wandered the busy streets of Kathmandu – sacred animals – had a rising sun painted on their sides, the symbol for the Communist Party of Nepal (United Marxist Leninists). Judging from the frequency of rising suns painted around the city, the communists appeared to have an edge in Kathmandu.

Prithivi Narayan Shah, the raja of the principality of Gorkha who had unified – or conquered – much of the present-day state of Nepal in 1767 and the founder of the Shah dynasty of the Nepalese monarchy, described his kingdom as a "garden of four castes and thirty-six tribes" to model the ethnic diversity and cohesion that he expected for the new state (Sharma 1992). By 1991 that garden seemed overgrown, like the one on the grounds of the Keshar Mahal, more robust branches choking off others by demanding most of its resources. In general, there was widespread discontent expressed with the domination by Pahari Brahmins and Chetris of most of the instruments of power: government, the civil service, education, and the military. The "thirty-six tribes" – the non-Hindu communities existing prior to the conquest that were erroneously dubbed "tribes" by the ruling elites – were particularly restless for change. Borrowing from the global discourses of the early 1990s, some began to describe these non-Hindu minorities (dubbed the *janajati*) as

Nepal's "indigenous" peoples in order to press for social change. Others attempted to form political parties to contest the elections on the basis of ethnic communalism. Significantly, the 1990 constitution forbade participation from explicitly communalist parties, fearing the same ethnic turmoil that at that time was tearing India apart. Concurrently, an effort to circumscribe state secularity was compromised in the same constitution by adding a comma after "Hindu" in a clause that initially read that Nepal was a "multi-lingual, multi-racial, Hindu monarchical state." In the first version only the monarchy was described as Hindu, and the fear was that the added comma implied that the Nepalese state itself, not just the monarchy, was Hindu. Critics charged that this was a result of the overrepresentation of Brahmins on the committee that drafted the constitution (Raeper and Hoftun 1992, 177).

It was the founder of the Rana lineage, Jang Bahadur Rana, who first wrote Nepal's current caste and ethnic categories into law, in the *muluki ain* (nation's code) of 1854, which rigidly assigned diminishing

Figure 2.1. Election banners on New Road, Kathmandu, April 1991.

rights and privileges to a hierarchical structure of Hindu and Buddhist castes, as well as to communities that followed both or neither religions. Brahmins and Chetris, priests and warriors, were at its apex, Hindu untouchables at its base; non-Hindu, alcohol-drinking Buddhist such as the Sherpas of Eastern Nepal, the Yolmo of Helambu, and the Tamang, who lived around the Kathmandu Valley, appear in the middle, ambiguous. Even though the revised *muluki ain* of 1962 appeared to remove official sanction for this hierarchy, it continued to reinforce traditional forms of Nepali culture, so that the linguistic, religious and cultural inequality of the original *muluki ain* became the weft on which the fabric of Nepalese life was woven. Many people from Helambu regard themselves as a non-Hindu *jati* (Sanskrit for "tribe," but generally taken to mean an ethnic group), thus reifying the political hierarchy of categories established by their conquerors.

The distinctions between discrete "tribal," caste, or cultural communities in Nepal are central to its sovereign order and frame most ethnological scholarship on the region, but they often take on different forms in daily life. John Whelpton (1997, 52), an independent scholar who writes extensively on Nepalese national identity, argues that most Nepalese do not make the distinction between caste and ethnic group (*jat* and *jati*, respectively) because, he argues, they "understand an important reality: the ethnic labels commonly employed often conceal internal differences and mask similarity between groups." The idea of a Helambu people, for example, masks internal divisions, such as those between the "lineage" and "reading" lamas that Graham Clarke (1980) describes in history, as well as between the lamas and the nonliterate peoples to whom they provided religious services. Communal politics in Nepal, then, is a modern phenomenon that challenges traditional hierarchy not by subverting the categories it imposed, but by empowering a persuasive identity that transformed those categories in practice.

That traditional hierarchy and what became of it are exemplified at Keshar Mahal. It is a display of power and knowledge that was, in retrospect, as anachronistic as the battered suits of medieval armour that flanked the sweeping staircase to the portrait gallery. The growling, glass-eyed Bengal tiger beside them is stuffed and covered with dust. Though numerous Nepali scholars continued to wring their hands over the possibility of a return to absolute monarchy for many years afterwards, its effective resurgence was, in retrospect, about as likely as the stuffed tiger leaping from its pose. But the ethnic categories that were codified by that monarchy and the widespread resentment of caste privilege were still stirring in the streets outside.

Paljor Lama was an attractive, charismatic, young schoolteacher and administrator I met through the Canadian NGO that organized my volunteer placement as a teacher at a Himalayan Trust-funded school in the Khumbu. Paljor, though, was from Helambu and was extremely cosmopolitan, to my knowledge speaking Yolmo, Tamang, Nepali, English, and some Danish. Hindi he knew from films, but he was well read in that language too. He frequently invited us to classical raga concerts or to feasts over which we lingered in conversation about music, politics, human rights, and others of his many passions. Sometimes he didn't show up for his own appointments, either because he was so busy elsewhere or he simply forgot.

The 1991 general election had created a near festive atmosphere throughout the Kathmandu valley, and few places were more festive than Paljor's house in Boudhanath, which buzzed with campaign activity. Paljor Lama's uncle, Nyima, was running in the election against a prominent member of the royalist Rastriya Prajanantra Party in Helambu Ward 3, a constituency about a two-day walk northeast of the city. Nyima was a successful entrepreneur, who owned a carpet factory and, at one point, an experimental tea plantation in Helambu. His opponent was the Keshar Rana's son.

Congress Party politics seemed to run deep in Paljor's family. Over bowls of his mother's delicious *thukpa* (Tibetan noodle soup) Paljor himself spoke of Mahatma Gandhi, Nehru, and BP Koirala as heroes. He was the first to teach me Nepali history. Koirala, he told us, was leader of the Nepali congress and elected prime minister before being dismissed in 1960, jailed, then exiled by then King Mahendra, and persecuted by his son, King Birendra, until his death in 1982. King Mahendra cited the incompetence of Koirala's government and the general divisive infighting between the political parties as the reason for establishing his partyless "panchayat" regime, which ensured that the monarchy would remain unchallenged by legitimate political forces. As both a leader of the 1950 revolution that overthrew the Rana regime in 1950 and a major literary figure during his exile in the 1960s, Koirala was an inspiration to the Congress-leaning pro-democracy movement and to many young, educated people like Paljor.

Though an ardent Congress Party supporter, Nyima Lama chose to run as an independent because he could not obtain the nomination for the Congress Party, which Paljor charged was due to the domination of the party by *Pahari* (hill or mountain) Brahmins and Chetris who dominated the emerging democratic parties as they had once dominated Rana-era Nepal. Paljor held the view that this domination needed to be addressed politically in the post *jan andolan* (people's movement) era and argued that the candidacy of his uncle, Nyima Lama, was intended to press the issue. As a Buddhist, Paljor regarded himself as fundamentally distinct from Hindu culture and, even though he professed to be admirer of BP Koirala and Gandhi, saw his own background as morally superior.

Once, a few years later when I told him that I had visited a Hindu friend's home for the annual Hindu Dasain festival, he was shocked: "Why would you go there? They kill animals only for the gods!" He was referring to the sacrifice of *boka* (non-castrated goats), the centrepiece ritual of a week of religious ceremony and feasting. Paljor told me (and this sentiment was frequently echoed by others with whom I spoke in Helambu) that the Buddhist rituals that they were forced by tradition to conduct at the same time as Dasain in Helambu were conceived to atone for the sins committed by the Hindus who occupied the lower valleys of the region, as they sacrificed for the festival.

Nyima's candidacy in the May election was also regarded as an assertion of ethnic autonomy through which the Helambu lamas, and perhaps the Buddhist janajati more generally, could challenge Brahmin and Chetris dominance of the political system.

Four years after the election of 1991, when I interviewed Nyima about the carpet industry, he proved to be unusually loquacious compared with most other men from Helambu that I met. He was also well schooled in the history of his people: "According to our belief, the Nyingmapa were chased away from Tibet and the fifth Buddha stayed in a cave [in] Helambu where there is a stupa now." The Nyingmapa is the oldest school of Tibetan Buddhism, which was persecuted in the past, sending religious refugees from the Tibetan plateau into the foothills of the Himalayas. Nyima referred to Padmasambhava, or Guru Rinpoche, as the "fifth Buddha." He went on:

> This was during the Malla period. The Lichhavi kings were also Buddhists. Like the Shah's family priest, at that time the Malla kings, and also the Lichhavi kings believed in tantric education. They liked our tantric customs. Rana people also admired our tantric education. Rana People gave guthi land and made a stupa for big lamas. Helambu people were

connected with the royal family, because the climate in Helambu is very nice. Helambu's girls were kept in the royal palace; they were very beautiful, and they were kept as servants during the Rana period and Shah period. They were kept inside. During the Rana period many of them were kept. We've now very good relation with them. There are still many hundreds of widows, queens from Helambu. But the Ranas have never accepted that Helambu is their parents-in-law's home. Helambu women were kept as servants but they became their wives. Babies were born, they are army officers now. But they treat us like Bhote or Madhesi. Anyone from the Tamang caste or other caste who are living around can't be in high position in army, they are in low position as a rule.

Nyima's historical narrative is mostly correct, corroborating, for example, Grahame Clarke's extensively documented, "A Helambu History" (1980). It is, however, the perspective he has on caste and ethnicity that is more significant here. Despite the close proximity of Helambu to a succession of rulers of Kathmandu, both in religion and by virtue of the extensive *guthi* lands (grants of land given to lama lineages that provide rich agricultural resources for the people of Helambu [see Regmi 1988]) that Kathmandu's rulers granted to them in exchange for ritual services, the Rana regimes arrogantly refused to acknowledge these historical bonds. They treated the people of Helambu as no better the Bhote or Madhesi, pejoratives for rude highlanders and lowland, *dhoti*-wearing peasants, respectively. As well, in the campaign in 1991 Nyima's electoral contest in Helambu Ward 3 was with a wealthy descendent of the ruling family that was partially subordinated during Nepal's first democratic revolution of 1951 (though they still held tight to the reins of power through the military and intermarriage with the ruling Shah clan of Nepal's king) and who stood to lose even more ground after the jan andolan.

Paljor asked if I would accompany him to Yangrima for the election as a sort of unofficial observer, warning me that the opposing candidate was going to attempt to intimidate people at the polling booth or encourage fraudulent voting. He reasoned with me that having a foreigner watch the polling process might discourage such behaviour, even though I was not an official international election observer. It was also unlikely that any official observers would be assigned to so remote and inconsequential a district. I agreed, eagerly, as this was an opportunity to peer into the backstage, to see beyond the symbols of an emerging democracy to the actual workings of political culture. It was also an opportunity to escape the heat and the tourists of Kathmandu.

Tridevi Marg still buzzed with activity in late April 1991, but Boudhanath – a predominantly Tibetan community several kilometres northeast of the city – seemed abandoned by those who lived there. Residence regulations meant that many of the people who lived and worked there, in carpet factories, restaurants, and tourist curio shops had to return to their native villages to vote. Indeed, life in Boudhanath nearly ground to a halt as almost everyone left for home to vote in the elections. On the morning of our departure I joined another Canadian volunteer teacher and two British "GAP" students, who also relished the opportunity to get out of dusty Kathmandu, where they taught in an English-language primary school at Nyima's house and carpet factory. We found three Mercedes buses parked outside that were teeming with people, already claiming seats or climbing onto the roof for the four-hour journey. Paljor met us and insisted that we ride inside and at the front of one of the buses in comparative comfort. The buses headed down Ring Road towards the western hills that surrounded the valley in a festive atmosphere. Seemingly everywhere, we passed processions of young people parading with flags and banners of Congress trees and Communist suns from other political parties. Young Lama supporters dangled dangerously from the open windows of the bus, insulting the passing processions then ducking back inside to the jovial approval of their friends before they could hear the fading response from outside.

As the dusty expanse of the Kathmandu Valley rolled away, we climbed through green terraces of rice paddies, bamboo thickets, and tamarind trees. When the convoy rounded Dulikhel with its breathtaking views of the central Himalayas, women and children scurried onto the highway before us laying out tall grasses to be threshed by our wheels, collecting the worked crop after we passed. Red-brick houses dotted the hillsides, many of them adorned with painted trees, suns, ploughs, and other symbols.

The buses turned onto a dirt road from the paved highway and lurched over a narrow bridge onto a potholed path towards Melemchi Pul. It was at this point that I was thankful that we were assigned seats at the front, as every pothole tossed the poor souls at the back two or three feet into the air, sometimes dashing their heads against the roof of the bus. It was stiflingly hot. As we had descended from the hills at Dhulikhel into Indrawati river valley, the atmosphere in the buses changed as the cool hill air ignited with heat and dust. Several people vomited out the windows into the dry paddies below. It was difficult to imagine a jeep making its way along such a road, let alone a Mercedes bus. Paljor tried to cheer us up by telling us that the locals named this "Noodle Highway" after the dried noodle company that reportedly paid for its construction in order to gain access to markets in the Himalayan interior. The road we were on, however, was a rough sort of social service.

Finally we reached a field of churned, dried mud that was the bus park at Melemchi Pul, a place that belied the romantic image of the Himalayan village: dilapidated stone cottages lining a garbage-strewn road and trees, filled not with Buddhist prayer flags, but with discarded plastic shopping bags. Two bridges on the river led to the footpaths into the hills that loomed overhead, the river bank covered with faeces. Once we had crossed the suspension bridge, the three-hour climb was welcome. When the trail levelled out after a couple of hours, we passed a large village that clung precariously to the side of the ridge and climbed again to a saddle between two hillocks with a small Buddhist stupa in the middle. This, I was to later learn, was Uttar Bhanjyang, where I was to return numerous times when I did fieldwork in the years to come. Its stupa also marked, more or less, the southern extent of the Helambu region. We reached Yangrima in darkness.

The lodge where we were staying also served as Nyima's election headquarters, and there was feverish activity all around. We were led into a back room where there was a fire to warm ourselves; even in May it was cool at night at this altitude. *Dal bhaat* was prepared for us, but the rice and lentils seemed to cook very slowly in their pressure cookers. *Raksi* – the traditional country liquor made from the distilled millet or rice beer which is imbibed in Helambu – was served and, since I had no food in my stomach, its effects went straight to my head. Paljor was discussing the campaign with some of the men who came in to speak with him and he translated for us what they said. They were expecting voting fraud at the polls the next day, and the opponent's workers had been observed handing out cash sums to villagers for their support – 2,000 rupees per vote was the figure he gave. Paljor regretted that Nyima could not offer anything like that sum, but told us that most of the people in Yangrima would not be swayed, as they were Helambu people and thus would automatically support Nyima. I noted that Paljor and the men he spoke with mentioned neither the Congress Party candidate nor the Communist candidate, who were also contesting the election in Helambu Ward 3. The race actually appeared to be between Nyima and the candidate from the Rastriya Prajantantra Party. I drank a container of treated water to forestall a hangover and retired to my bed.

I awoke the next morning to the thunder of hundreds of feet stampeding across the wooden floors below. I dressed and went back down to the kitchen, looking for Paljor. He was not to be found, but the young woman who seemed to be the cook for the swelling numbers of people in the lodge handed me a cup of freshly churned salt tea with her fair hands blackened with ash. I drank it gratefully, as the morning was also damp and the stone walls of the lodge retained the chill long after the sun had risen. With still no sign of Paljor, I struck up a conversation with a teenager named Phurba, a graduate of the English Boarding School who spoke English. He was incredibly energetic, frenetic even, as he spoke about the campaign and how he was expecting trouble from Rana's *goonda* – gangs of boys and young men that were used by all political parties to protect their candidate and intimidate the supporters of others. "But I am ready," he said, partially opening his jacket to reveal a large Nepali *khukri* tucked into his trousers. It was sheathed, but I had seen the uniquely curved knives used many times before in their many domestic applications: peeling potatoes, cutting rope, and opening cans. I had also been told, however, that the small semi-circular gap cut into the blade where it connects to the wooden handle is an intentional design feature that diverted an enemy's polluting blood off the blade before it contaminated the triumphant hand of the person wielding it. The khukri is an artefact of both Nepal's violent martial past and its cultural obsession with caste purity, an obsession that is a political construct amplified by Nepal's Rana rulers.

Paljor finally arrived, having slept late, and we were joined by the two GAP volunteers. After tea, Paljor suggested that we walk up the hill to one of the village's two gonpa, which was serving today as a polling station. As we stepped out onto the path, an army helicopter, flying so low that its wake aroused the prayer flags that stood in front of every house, swept across the millet fields. Radio Nepal had reported that the interim government was expecting election-day violence, not only between cadres of the various political parties but even, perhaps more seriously, from those opposed to the elections and having an interest in seeing them disrupted. The army had been mobilized and all public transportation had been shut down, measures to ensure that voting fraud and ballot box theft could be minimized. The olive green helicopter race overhead was a sure sign to all that this was not an ordinary day and that the state could reach even such a remote place when it so desired.

The gonpa square was already crowded with people as we arrived and the voting had started. Paljor went on ahead to the polling booth while the two GAP volunteers and I remained behind. We stood together at the back of the square in the glaring sun, watching as people queued in an orderly fashion to vote. This behaviour was unusual in itself, as I had rarely seen a Nepalese queue so respected; in Kathmandu at least, even getting on a bus is a chaotic, first-come, first-served free-for-all. As I marvelled over it, I noticed a bag hanging on the side of a shed facing the square, out of which protruded the unmistakable black handle of a khukri. I was initially alarmed, but then realized that the bag belonged to one of the elderly women sitting under the shed to keep out of the sun. The khukri was more likely to be used to chop onions, I reasoned, than to confront a political cadre.

I took a photograph of the women and was just replacing the lens cap when a cloud of dust arose from the queue in front of us. The orderly crowd had burst into motion. As I turned the camera towards the event, people screamed. A group of young men sitting on the compound wall rose to their feet, pointing and shouting to someone in the crowd. The crowd surged in the centre and, as if propelled by centrifugal force, people ran in all directions away from the melee. A wooden bench flew into the air and was then reabsorbed into the crowd. A sudden silence fell, as if the flying bench itself had exuded some power over the crowd, the dust settled, the men on the wall sat back down and the queue reformed, as if a storm had passed.

Paljor came back to join us wearing a broad, white smile. I asked him what had happened. "Some people thought that there was some cheating," he said. Those at the front of the queue were given a bottle of ink by someone and they prematurely dipped their fingers in as a sign that they had voted. When they reached the table to receive their ballot, they were turned away, as their fingers were already dyed blue. This procedural gaffe led to accusations from Nyima's supporters that it was Rana's supporters who had sent the ink bottle up the line to orchestrate these refusals, which was what had caused the "confusion." "But who threw the bench?" I asked. "Oh, that was me," he chuckled. "Phurba got into an argument with someone from Rana's people and tried to throw a bench at them. I took it from him, but it flipped up into the air and fell on some people. They are alright, but everyone was a little bit scared." He then suggested that we go and have some tea before we set

Figure 2.2. The voting queue at Yangrima, April 1991. Near the centre of the image Paljor can be seen wrestling the bench from one of Nyima's supporters.

off for another polling station that he needed to visit in the afternoon. I was thankful that Phurba had somehow forgotten about the khukri under his jacket.

At the end of voting, the ballot boxes were sealed and then taken, under police escort, to Melemchi Pul for transport to Chauthara, the district headquarters of Sindupalchok district, where they would be unsealed and counted. The level of security I saw everywhere was accompanied by a general apprehension about the fairness of the election. In 1980 a national referendum on ending the partyless panchayat leadership system was lost by the agitating political parties in an election that was widely thought to have been rigged by the monarchist forces, and people now feared the same outcome in 1990. The following morning Paljor and his election volunteers followed the ballot boxes down to Melemchi Pul. When we arrived, we found the narrow streets crammed with people, huddled around transistor radios and holding heated conversations. Blue-shirted police carried frayed bamboo *lathi* (batons) for crowd control, and for the first time we saw soldiers in combat uniforms with rifles casually shouldered, forcing their faces closer to the many radios that various groups of men huddled around. A particularly large crowd had surrounded the government offices beyond the muddy bus park, there was furious shouting, and both police and soldiers were holding the throngs away from two blue pickup trucks parked in front. I turned to Paljor to ask him what this furore was all about, but he had disappeared, leaving his volunteers stranded in the crowd.

Passing through the bus park, we noticed that the buses were neatly positioned and did not have their engines idling, as was usually the case. They also were ominously empty. I asked someone standing outside a bus in my best but pathetic Nepali if the buses were leaving for Kathmandu. He glared at me, as if my attempt to speak in Nepali was not welcome. "Today, no bus!" he shouted. We volunteers looked at each other in horror; two of them were scheduled to fly to New Delhi the next day, and I was to leave for Bangkok the day after. We simply had to get to Kathmandu that night. We redoubled our efforts to find Paljor. One of the GAP students spotted him crouched with some others around a radio.

We approached him but were silenced and directed to listen to the broadcast, which, of course, we could not understand. An announcement was made, Paljor slapped the side of his face in shock, and a chorus of cheers and shouts arose from the crowd all over town. We later learned that preliminary results had been announced: the leader of the Congress Party and interim prime minister Krishna Bhattarai had lost his own seat in Kathmandu to the leader of the Communist Party of Nepal (United Marxist-Leninist), Madan Bhandari. This was perhaps the most significant single constituency in Nepal, a contest between two leading figures of the pro-democracy movement. Bhandari took the precaution of running in two constituencies, an unusual practice allowed under the new constitution, as he did not expect to win against the Congress Party leader. Bhattarai had not done the same and thus could not continue as prime minister, even though his party went on to win the election overall.

Our panic about getting back to Kathmandu dulled our appreciation of this moment, and we pressed Paljor about transportation. He told us not to worry and slipped back into the crowd. We did not see him again for another four hours.

They Kill Animals Only for the Gods

The crowd at the government office grew larger, but less volatile, as they passively watched ballot boxes being loaded into the closely guarded pickup trucks. As election results from Kathmandu were being announced on Radio Nepal, the ballot boxes from Helambu Ward 3 remained sealed and were bouncing along the "noodle highway" to Chautara to be counted. It occurred to us that we could walk down the same road to the main highway and somehow hire a private vehicle back to Kathmandu, as Paljor was not forthcoming with transportation. The two GAP volunteers, much younger and not wishing to risk getting stuck in the dark (a likelihood, given that it was already late afternoon) chose to remain behind and find Paljor, but I decided, along with another Canadian volunteer, to start walking. As we walked, my anxiety grew. Sindhupalchok is not a favoured trekking destination and the crowds at Melemchi Pul had been menacing, which I feared characterized many of the people in this impoverished and unwelcoming valley.

About an hour after we set off, the sun was setting and bathed the valley and hills in a golden glow that at any other time would have been spectacular, but now only amplified my anxiety. Then a mammoth truck, such as those used to move heavy earth, roared up the hill, forcing us to dive into the scrub at the side of the road. It came to an abrupt stop ahead. Paljor climbed over the massive metal walls of the truck and motioned for us to get in. He had arranged transport, he told us, but it would cost us each 100 rupees. We climbed in and found the two GAP volunteers sitting on their packs, surrounded by ten to fifteen armed policemen perched on their helmets and playing cards. The truck lurched over the potholes of the road, throwing us against its formidable sides, and everyone began to laugh, relieved perhaps, to be leaving Melemchi Pul. About an hour later the truck stopped for fuel. A few of the policemen managed to get me to part with another 100 rupees, ran into a local "cold store" (shop with refrigerator) and emerged with several large bottles of Star beer. The final leg of the journey turned into something of a party as the beer was consumed and the policemen began alternately to drink and to sing. Finally, the truck pulled to a stop, and the policemen stood up, put on their helmets, and shouldered their rifles or drew their lathi. The gate of the truck opened to fog mingled with the smell of smoke and burning rubber. The policemen took off into the night, bellowing commands, chants, and catcalls. Several fires burned in the emptied streets. Through the smoke, we located a taxi, and took it back to Paljor's home.

My sleep that night was disturbed not only by the usual howling of wild dogs, but by a platoon of young men I could hear through the darkness, double stepping through the narrow pathways between the brick houses, chanting political slogans, and thrusting their fists into the night to celebrate the victory of Madan Bhandari and the CPN (UML) against the KP Bhattarai and the Congress Party. Their passion, their discipline, and their aggressiveness was chilling. After 12 May 1991 the fragile coalition that was triumphant during the jan andolan would fracture and begin a social and political devolution that grew more chaotic in the years to follow, as if it had unleashed a pent-up destructive power. These political changes threatened to put to an end to the myth of Nepal as a "zone of peace" populated by impoverished, compliant people who followed their traditions conservatively.

From the vantage point of that first election in 1991, I began a relationship with a series of places – Tridevi Marg, Boudhanath, Helambu – and with the people who lived in them that would unfold over the next decade, reflecting the then uncertain changes that we all knew would come. Though this political evolution was never a central focus of the research that I was to do over the next ten years, it was a constant backdrop for it. Politics, whether democratic, revolutionary, or ethnic, continued to impose itself on my ability to conduct research in other areas, just as it imposed itself on the lives of those whom I worked with. Witnessing the election in Yangrima was to observe something of the ordinary in contemporary Nepali life. I had begun to realize that changes were afoot, and that the pace of them was unpredictable and perhaps beyond anyone's control. Alexis de Tocqueville (1990, 7), an early admirer of democracy, remarked that effective democracy has to be guided by "the moral classes." In the absence of such guidance, the democratic movement is "abandoned to its wildest instincts" and lost to the "vices and wretchedness" of the streets. Street demonstrations and *chakka jam* (lit. wheel stoppages, or traffic disruptions) were to become an ordinary, daily, almost mundane reality for my Nepali friends, intruding frequently in their lives and, arguably, impeding Nepal's fragile social progress.

A few months after I returned to Canada, I learned that Nyima Lama was defeated handily by the Rana candidate and was outpolled as well by the local Communist. He went on to contest the next two elections, this time under the Congress Party banner, but Rana was able to retain his seat each time. This success was taken as evidence by Nyima and Paljor that nothing much had changed in 1991 – the old order continued to fend off democratic challenges to its power and privilege. A decade later, the same sense of grievance was successfully taken up by the Maoist insurgents.

In a recent review, James Fisher (2007), a prominent American anthropologist with many years of experience in the Nepal Himalaya, pointed out that for the most part anthropologists have been caught unawares by Nepal's political turmoil in recent years. Their focus on narrowly defined questions of culture and their predisposition to study the rural, the idyllic, the exotic have, he charged, prevented them from engaging in historical prediction. It could be argued that anthropology was never intended to be a predictive science, and that the "wildest instincts" of mass change are difficult for anyone to predict, except in hindsight. Nevertheless, Fisher's charge is not so easily dismissed. My "observation" of the 1991 election was a glimpse of some of the tensions and internal antagonisms that were being set free by the collapse of monarchical authority. Though I could not yet call myself an anthropologist, it was both a formative engagement with places and people who would become more important as the years went by and the point at which I entered an emerging understanding of myself as an anthropologist in these places and with these people.

Chapter Three

A Map of Boudhanath

In 1994, three years after my time as a volunteer teacher, dharma student, and unofficial election observer, I returned to Nepal to begin research on Tibetan carpet production for my PhD in anthropology. In the interim, the carpet industry had transformed the square that surrounds the enormous stupa with the Tibetan name *byarung khashor* (lit. "permission once given, cannot be taken back"). During my previous visit, the city of Kathmandu seemed to end abruptly at Chabahil, about three kilometres west of the stupa, from where I walked across green fields of ripening rice, punctuated by intermittent cottages and temples that stretched almost as far as the stupa square. Three years later large tenement buildings had been erected on these fields, along with towering monasteries and factory buildings. Where there weren't buildings, there were stacks of bricks and piles of cement and rusting rebar. The peaceful atmosphere of Boudhanath, if it ever had existed as anything more than travellers' nostalgia, had been transformed by tourism, foreign capital, and modern economic development.

This is where I chose to do fieldwork. After about a month of paying tribute to immigration and university bureaucrats, looking up old friends, and spending time fruitlessly trying to discuss my project with state officials, I faced the cold prospect of beginning my research with the people who really mattered, the people who lived in the tangle of tenements that was now Boudhanath. For a few days I walked through this jungle of concrete, hearing Tibetan chants and the ubiquitous metallic tapping that I would soon discover were thousands of young carpet weavers driving down with flat-headed hammers the metal bars that their carpets were looped around. I frequently became lost, finding myself at a dead end or driven by dogs to change direction.

Monsoon downpours forced me under trees or into vestibules. Walking along the only paved road in the area – which I later learned was paved to accommodate traffic to one of Nepal's largest carpet factories – I noticed that the density of buildings began to thin. Rice paddies and a few remaining cottages, surrounded by carefully tended flower and vegetable gardens, suggested an earlier, pastoral time. Crumbling Rana-era buldings sent aged bricks into the muddy roads. At an intersection there stood a towering pipal tree adorned with prayer flags and vermilion powder, once an indication to pilgrims climbing down from the northern hills that the stupa was only a little further. At the tree I turned to see an astonishing view of Boudhanath, which lifted me over the urban mayhem below, allowing me to see its contours and patterns. In the middle stood byrarung khashor, its half-closed eyes staring back at me.

Mary Louise Pratt (1992) wrote of the obsession that colonial agents and travellers had with "promontory descriptions," the "monarch-of-all-that-I-survey" trope that characterized colonial accounts of subaltern places. From this vantage point, I conceived the task of creating my own "promontory description" – of mapping roads and alleys and identifying carpet factories so that I could systematically begin to investigate the industry and the community that it was embedded in. Looking down on the bright, new tenements that lined the twisted roadways, I saw parallels between my own need to model the landscape and the needs of colonial agents in the past to map, classify, and impose order on the worlds they were to govern. Not that I wanted to rule this landscape, but I did want to extract from it knowledge that would be an accurate representation of space and what lay in it.

It occurred to me that maps of the area ought to exist already. I searched some of the better bookstores and government publication outlets in Kathmandu, the British Library, and the Canadian Cooperation Office. In the most recent topographic map I found of the Kathmandu Valley, only the stupa square and the paved road that passes Boudhanath on its way from Kathmandu to Sankhu were detailed. Other than the cluster of buildings immediately around the stupa, only a few scattered dwellings were indicated and none of the many roads and paths that now existed. On the tourist maps that were readily available in the tourist hub in Thamel, Boudhanath was indicated by a crude sketch of the stupa that filled the entire upper right-hand side of the map, the cartographer apparently thinking that this would be the only feature a foreigner would be interested in.

Figure 3.1. The Boudhanath stupa, byrarung khashor, July 1994.

Every weekday morning, for the first four months of my fieldwork, I climbed into a cramped, Indian-made, three-wheeled tempo and travelled from Boudhanath to Naya Bazar, another comparatively recent neighbourhood that had sprung up along the Ring Road near Thamel, for Nepali language lessons. During one of those lessons, I asked my teacher, Shyam Pradhan, where I could find a recent, accurate map of the Boudhanath. After our lesson, on his suggestion, we set off for the Kathmandu municipal building on Dharma Path. Once inside the crumbling nineteenth-century Rana mansion that served as municipal offices, I watched as Shyam deferentially introduced me to a city official and handed over a letter of introduction that I had obtained from the Social Sciences and Humanities Research Council (SSHRC) of Canada, which was funding my research. The official studied it carefully, smiled at me, but then asked Shyam for a point of clarification. Both men hovered over the letter, pointing with their fingers at the letterhead and the signatures, mapping, as it were, its significance. Finally the city official nodded and disappeared into a back room. In his absence, a peon appeared with a pot of sugary tea and poured two glasses for us. We waited. The official finally appeared, triumphant, from the back room, and handed me a map of plans for a German garbage removal program that showed much detail on recent road and building construction. I studied the map as we left the building and discovered, when we were back on the pungent street, that it covered only the area inside the Ring Road that circled the city. Boudhanath, even though politically part of the Municipality of Kathmandu, was not part of its garbage renewal scheme or even on its own map.

It struck me as odd, and significant, that I was unable to obtain a detailed map of Boudhanath, that such a social representation was unavailable or at least very hard to find. Maps are an essential tool of modern governance, indeed, of modernity itself. Timothy Mitchell (2000) observed that maps of space as well as the statistical images of the social constructed through the national census (both aided and abetted by the social sciences) are essential tools for the experience of contemporaneity or the sense that one exists in a homogeneous world that is moving away, sequentially, from the past to an unfulfilled future. What did it mean, then, that I could not locate an accurate, contemporary map of the bustling peri-urban community of Boudhanath? Without such basic knowledge, how could mail be delivered, garbage collected, or voters lists be created? How could the modern democracy that Nepal was aspiring to become be effective? Benedict Anderson (1991) noted the role that map making played in constructing modern empires, by placing disparate peoples in a "colonial-era bird's eye atlas" that forged "imagined communities" of subjugated populations. The absence of a detailed map of Boudhanath suggested that Boudhanath was regarded as a place that was not yet a part of contemporary Kathmandu.

Shyam told me that Boudhanath had always been regarded as a distinct, and slightly suspect, place by the residents of Kathmandu, at least those who lived within the boundaries of the Ring Road. Twenty years ago, he said, you could not even convince a taxi to take you there, as drivers feared Boudhanath's unsavoury reputation for violence and prostitution. The situation was different now, of course, as not only had the stupa become one of the Kathmandu Valley's major tourism and pilgrimage destinations, but the community around it had become a focal point for Tibetans and Sherpas who migrated to the valley to work in the tourism and carpet industries. None of the development I was seeing in the area was mapped, so I could conclude only that the hastily built houses and tenements, as well as the new roads paved with recently crushed masonry, were the product of unplanned and unregulated development. Shyam said that this could not be so, because new land was being sold in Boudhanath, particularly along the Dhobi Kola valley behind it, and the area was teeming with new houses. He suggested that we try the government land office in Chabahil for a map of the area, one that would provide an accurate representation of the many new roads and residential communities that I needed to become familiar with.

The next day Shyam and I took a tempo up to the land office in Chabahil after our Nepali language lesson. At this stage, I was only too happy to have Shyam's help, as my Nepali skills were minimal. I was particularly happy that he was there to face the stern-looking men in the land office. Once again my letter from the SSHRC was produced as well as a letter of introduction that I had received, appropriately stamped, from Tribhuvan University, where I was registered as a research student. Stamps legitimate important cultural capital in Nepal: unless a letter or document is stamped, it has little value. Once again the letters were studied intently while tea was served by an older man in a beat-up topi and ragged trousers. Shyam explained what I was looking for and we were directed to a large leather portfolio that lay on a table beside us. As he opened it, the Land Office employee told Shyam that these maps might not be particularly helpful to us. Shyam translated his warning as I opened the portfolio to study the map, which was an abstract collage of irregular shapes and measurements that were coded, but not related to any recognizable feature – a road, river, or even the stupa square. They were land lots, geometric packages of value that oriented the reader not to the landscape that I saw from my balcony and walked through each day, but to the dissolution of that landscape into privately owned, fungible fiefdoms. It struck me that the lack of any other detail in the map, if not intentional, then was passively deliberate. For of what relevance is a landscape with its inscribed meanings, stupas, temples, shrines, and trees, to the logic of commoditization? Zygmunt Bauman (1997, 34) remarks that modern power rests initially on the orderly mapping of space in such a way that it deprives local orientations and then on the reconfiguration of space to fit "the degree of perfection previously seen only on the drawing board." In that sense, this particular map was an accurate blueprint for the transformation of Boudhanath, in that it facilitated the commoditization of land for private dwellings, industry, and tourism and disrupted traditional patterns of land use and inheritance. That this representation was readable solely to a trained eye suggests that the process of transformation itself was a matter of concern only for commercial elites.

If I were to use a map of Boudhanath for my research, I would have to make one. For the next two months, I spent my mornings in language study and afternoons wandering the roads and footpaths of Boudhanath, observing and marking features in a small black book and noting signs of carpet production that were everywhere apparent. In a brick plaza behind the rice paddy were a row of metal shutters that opened intermittently to reveal a single upright loom, a wooden plank underneath providing a seat for a row of three young weavers at work, oblivious to the traffic on the road outside. I watched as they worked, their hands blurred as they wove, stopping occasionally to hammer down the iron rod they wove around to join the completed pile, wool dust floated in the air. One of them looked at me and I moved on. Each afternoon I walked over an area of about 10 square kilometres that surrounded my flat, sketching roads, footpaths, potential factories, and other features in my notebook. Its pages were so small that the sketches spilled over to the next page, and arrows and codes began to indicate how it all could be reconnected once I returned and recorded my observations on a master map that lay on a makeshift drawing board in my flat.

Local people began to notice me walking back and forth through the area, stopping to scratch notes from time to time, poking my head around corners, studying the goings on inside walled compounds. A small group of children who played regularly at a construction site were the first to notice my regular wanderings. One afternoon, one of them ran up to me, shook my pant leg, and bellowed, "Hello, hello, *gu ko dhalo* (lit. "balls of shit)!" He ran back to his friends, all of whom were giggling furiously. At the time, my language skills were insufficient to make out what they said, but I was glad to be noticed and wrote down the phrase to ask Shyam about later. It also occurred to me that my regular presence on this particular road was somewhat unusual, since, while many foreign tourists regularly visited the stupa square about ten minutes away, few ever wandered this far from its restaurants and curio shops. If tourists who visited Boudhanath were aliens, I was even more of an alien, as my presence was long term and my wandering gaze directed at things that most foreigners were not interested in.

The central point of my map was the Boudhanath stupa, which was surrounded by a brick square that was crumbling from the weight of thousands of Buddhist pilgrims who circumambulated it, spinning the tin prayer wheels that were embedded in its walls as they went. Just outside its southern shrine was the main gate and beyond that the potholed road that leads from Kathmandu to Sundarijal. At this point traffic was always bumper to bumper, as buses, taxis, tourists, and enormous lorries jostled in a throng of roadside markets, vegetable stands, and other shops that sold bolts of bright cloth, furniture, prayer flags, and Buddhist statuettes. Bicycle-wallahs with baskets of fresh fruit chanted their wares to passers-by, and boys chased people down the muddy sidewalk offering to shine boots, shoes, sneakers, and sandals. For a few paise you could be weighed by a ragged girl carrying a common bathroom scale. Within the stupa square itself, people moved clockwise, always clockwise. Busloads of Japanese, Korean, Chinese, and Indian tourists joined the Tibetans already there; young Westerners climbed onto the stupa itself to take photographs; others haggled with shop owners over masks, drums, religious paintings, or antique carpets. Under a makeshift tarpaulin roof, several children lined up rows of Hindi-language comic books, offering other children an opportunity to read them for a few paise. At dusk this throng grew into massive procession of Tibetan and other Buddhist Nepalis lighting lamps fuelled by rancid butter, making offerings at the shrine to Ajima, the goddess of smallpox located at the northern base of the stupa. Byrarung khashor overlooked this scene and remained indifferent to the development going on around it.

From the stupa square roads and footpaths radiate in every direction, revealing more shops and markets, schools, and, of course, a number of garishly adorned Buddhist monasteries that served both Nepalese Buddhists and the prominent, infrequently restive Tibetan refugee population. Though Tibetan Buddhists – in which I include Nepalese co-religionist Sherpa and Yolmo peoples – are a minority in Nepal, and likely a minority in this community as well, their culture dominates Boudhanath. By walking these roads and footpaths, the powerful connection between the Tibetan Buddhist community and the carpet industry was made apparent (Gombo 1985). Just outside the main gate to the square was the Sherpa Sewa Samhiti, the recently constructed large monastic-style building that served the Solu-Khumbu Sherpa community. Across the road was the Boudhanath Handicraft Centre, the oldest carpet factory in the area, partly owned by the Tibetan

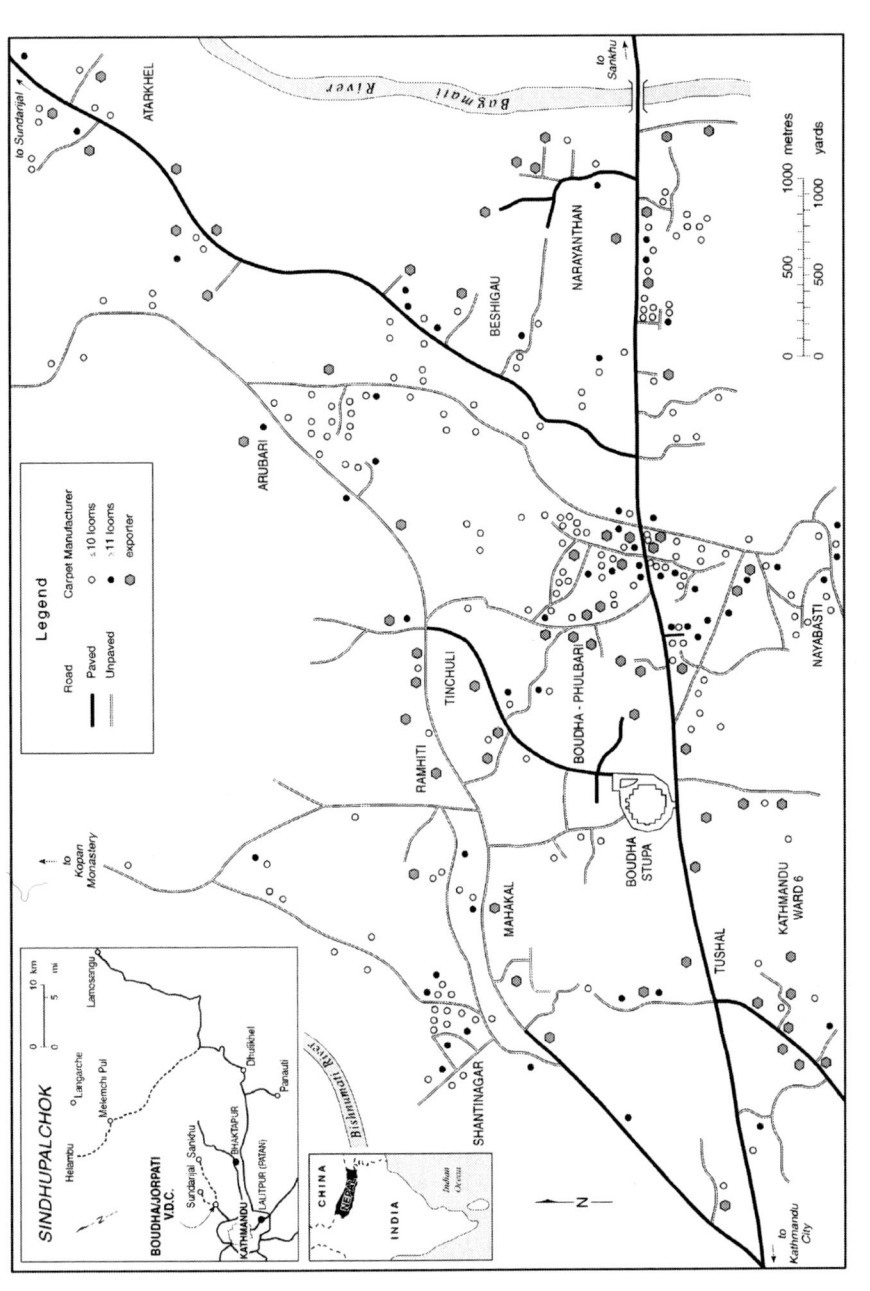

Figure 3.2. Sketch map of Boudhanath, Ward 9, and the Jorpati Village Development Committee in October 1995, showing carpet manufactories surveyed. Cartography by Loris Gasparotto.

Government in Exile in India. Along the street, several shops catered to carpet producers and weavers, selling wool, looms, and tools, while other shops sold carpets, 120 cm × 150 cm *khaden* carpets that showed traditional Tibetan design elements. These, I would learn, were considered inferior, local-market carpets woven with Indian wool, not the export-grade Tibetan carpets that were woven with wool that was an mixture of Tibetan and New Zealand wool, usually in abstract open-field designs. Other than these shops, there were few indications of the massive carpet industry immediately around the stupa square. It was along the side roads that led south of the main road and the square itself, particularly the footpaths of adjacent Jorpati, where the industry was ubiquitous. Almost every other building was a carpet factory, in storefront shops, the ground floors of houses, cottages, and tenements. Many of the people circling the stupa in the evening were carpet entrepreneurs and weavers, for whom walking around the stupa was not only of religious significance, but social as well. It was a chance to meet friends, flirt, gossip, receive news from home, and also share information about employment or carpet orders.

The contrast between the Tibetan pilgrims spinning prayer wheels as they walked around the stupa and me, a researcher obsessively plotting their community on graph paper, rests on how and where we move. In Bauman's dystopian interpretation of modernity, it is mobility, the freedom of people to go where they want when they want, that marks elite status. For Bauman, tourists "move out of the locality – any locality – at will," while locals "watch helplessly the sole locality they inhabit moving away from under their feet" (1998, 18). As Bauman suggests, we tourists, anthropologists, NGO staff, human-rights workers, global merchants, diplomats, and soldiers are parvenus, someone in a place but not of it. Though we all are in other places for various reasons – conducting research; attempting to make the world a better place; making money; consuming experience or, for that matter, masks, drums, religious paintings, and antique carpets – what we share is the fact that we are free to travel in the first place. Our presence in their landscape is a poignant reminder to them that they are not.

One afternoon, a group of young boys approached and begged for money. I repeated one of the first phrases that Shyam had taught me (following a curriculum he had developed for teaching American Embassy staff): "*Maagnu hudaaina*" (You shouldn't beg). The boys repeated, "*Hudaaina? Hudaaina? Hunchha! Hunchha!*" (We should! We should!).

They chanted this repeatedly, and I joined in, much to their amusement. They walked along with me for a while, then one of them again called out, "Hello, hello, *gu-ko dhalo!*" after which they ran off, giggling. Despite my daily Nepali language lessons, I still could not make out what this meant. I was finding acquiring a second language at my age somewhat daunting, even though Nepali is an Indo-European language with a fairly clear structure and a minimum of tongue-twisting phonemes to master.

Later that week, Shyam joined me on my afternoon walkabout. We covered the dusty distance from Paljor's house in Chabahil to Jorpati and afterwards paused for a cold beer at our favourite local haunt near the stupa square. It occurred to me to ask Shyam what *gu ko dhalo* meant. He face turned red and he muttered, *"badmas keta"* (naughty boys). I repeated this to him, and he corrected me, *"Nay, badmas."* It was difficult for my tongue to distinguish between a retroflex *t* and a dental *d*, and, as a result, I had inadvertently called the boys soy beans. But they were naughty, Shyam corrected. I asked him again what *gu ko dhalo* meant. "It doesn't mean anything, it is nonsense language, children's language," he said.

I pressed him until he finally, reluctantly admitted, "It means shit. Balls of shit." *Gu ko dhalo*. In Nepali, *dhalo* (ball) rhymes with "hello," and so this was an innocent scatological rhyme that children all over the world indulge in. Or was it? Shyam insisted that the boys had not intended any disrespect or insult, they were playing a trick on me simply because it could be played. As a foreigner, I could not understand the implications of their taunt and was thus not in a position to scold them for it. It occurred to me, however, that this particular linguistic performance was more than mere youthful tomfoolery, that is, because it was a specific mode of discourse, between a local Nepali speaker and a global English speaker. Their mischief would make no sense in Nepali alone; it was rhyme across two languages, a streetwise critique of global mobility. It had a levelling effect on me, because it made my presence on their streets an absurdity. The American sociologist William Corsaro (Corsaro and Molinari 2008) writes about how his linguistic incompetence levels him in the eyes of the Italian school children he studies. He is not a child, but also not quite an adult, and thus he is permitted to participate in aspects of child culture normally closed to adults. My own childlike abilities in spoken Nepali were being perceived not only by children. Though speaking English is a sign of being highly educated, modern, and "developed," my daily attempts to speak and comprehend Nepali marked me as an even stranger stranger, one who was straying uncharacteristically far from the shops and restaurants of the stupa square.

The factory at the end of the road I was on was one of the oldest, largest, and most influential in the Kathmandu Valley. From a distance, it looked like a combination of Bentham's panopticon and Dracula's castle – three towering, windowless, red-brick buildings in a circle, facing inwards, behind a stone wall protected by sharp, broken glass cemented on top to keep intruders out, or prisoners in. Between the towers, I could see ropes drying laundry and lines of Tibetan prayer flags dancing in the breeze. In front there was an enormous steel door, rusted red, crowned with sharp spikes of metal, and a man wearing a comically oversized police cap balancing on a wooden chair.

This was the *palé*, one of the security guards who stood vigil outside the larger carpet factories to supervise who went in and who went out. They often exuded an inflated sense of self-importance, as oversized as their uniforms, much like security guards almost anywhere else. Nevertheless, the palé was an important person to get on the right side of, as no one entered a factory without his permission. One of my first attempts to approach a carpet manufacturer for my study was at this factory located along the banks of Bagmati River in Jorpati, a factory that had an extremely negative reputation among weavers, subcontractors, and even other export manufacturers. They called it "the German factory," as it was owned by a Nepalese woman who was married to a prominent German carpet importer. I knew this as I approached the gate and supposed that I would not be welcome there. To my surprise, the palé lazily nodded as I gestured towards the gate, as if he were expecting me.

Once inside, I was immediately stopped by several men who asked what I was doing. In the inadequate Nepali I spoke at the time I explained that I wanted to speak with the saahuji, and I presented my card and a letter of introduction I had received from the office of the Central Carpet Industries Association (which I hoped would make for easy passage into places such as this). One of the men gently took the letter from my hands and disappeared up a flight of iron steps. He returned after a few minutes and explained in equally inadequate English that the saahuji was with a client, but that he would be with me shortly. The men then smiled and left me alone with the palé, who stared at me for a few moments and, as if losing interest, wandered away.

I waited on my own for the saahuji to appear. From inside, I could see that the towers that could be seen from the street were worker's dormitories. I could hear the whistle of pressure cookers and smell dal being cooked. I waited, ignored by people bustling about me. After a few minutes had passed, I found a concrete step to sit on and made a few jottings in my notebook, trying to recall a discussion I had had a few hours earlier. After even more time had passed, I rose to stretch my legs and through a window beside me noticed some rolled-up carpets .

At that point, the palé sprang from his chair and pushed me back through the gate, which he slammed after me. He glared through the barred window, pushed back his ersatz military cap, and turned away. Confused and incensed, I stared dumbly at the closed door. After a few minutes another man, wearing a sheepish smile appeared at the door and told me abruptly that the saahuji was away on holiday and that I should return in a few days. Apparently, he had finished his discussions with his client and set out on vacation as I waited. The man passed the ineffective introduction letter back to me and the gate was slammed once more.

At the time, I wondered if it was a mistake to jot down notes or to appear to the palé to be snooping around, as it aroused his suspicions about what I was there to find. He was likely used to foreigners arriving at his gates, as visits by European buyers must have been fairly common, but they usually arrived by taxi or company vehicle. I had approached on foot, carrying a small knapsack filled with books and papers. I left the way I came, walking down the potholed road back to Jorpati Chowk.

I never returned to the "German factory." I did hear about it often, from many different people throughout my fieldwork: stories of labour disputes, violence, exploitation, child labour, and racketeering. The German factory epitomized the image of a Nepalese carpet factory then prevalent in many people's minds, both in Nepal and in Europe, where the bulk of Tibetan hand-knotted carpets were sold. It was forbidding, sinister, and prison like. It also represented, for me, the fear that I had chosen my field poorly. I feared that carpet factories were closed to outside scrutiny and therefore likely the morally corrupt places that people imagined them to be.

One evening my telephone rang. This was a shock, as I had been making outgoing calls for several weeks but until now no one had called me. I picked up the receiver and it crackled, sounding like the call was coming from across an ocean. A deep, heavily accented voice told me that he was someone named Dorje Lama. I didn't recognize the name. Dorje told me that we had met in Nayabasti a few days earlier, and that he had my telephone number written on the back of my business card. I had been handing out these cards quite freely in the past few days as I introduced myself to people in carpet factories, and I recalled that a few requested that I write my Boudhanath number on the back. Dorje invited me to interview him in his factory and dictated directions to find it. His voice was distant, barely audible, but I recorded the directions as best I could.

The next morning I set off for Nayabasti, where I thought Dorje and I had met on the porch of a large stucco house that my notes recorded as belonging to a Mingmar Lama. I traced Dorje's directions on the map and eventually located a large brick building with barred windows. Inside were rows of industrial carpet looms, steel frames with adjustable brackets to stretch the warp to most buyer-preferred sizes. Weavers sat on wooden planks underneath, three to a loom. There was no light other than what came through the barred window and the atmosphere was permeated with a strong smell of urine. I went to the door and knocked. The weavers looked sleepily towards me and went back to their work. I called out, *"Saahuji hunu hunchha?"* One of the weavers replied, *"Hunu hunna."* By now, a crowd of onlookers had assembled, studying me. One boy stepped forward; he was well dressed, neatly groomed, and spoke passable English. He asked what I wanted, and I explained that I was looking for the saahuji, Dorje Lama, as we had an appointment. He translated this through the door and received a response only slightly more elaborate than the one I had received. "The saahuji is not here, sir," he reported.

"I know, but can they tell us when he will return?" This was repeated to the weavers, who shook their heads. "He will be back soon," the boy told me, though I did not know how he could know this from their response to his question. "Perhaps we can wait a while and come back when he returns. Please, my room is just there," he pointed across the street. "I would very much like to help you." Reluctantly, I was led across the dusty road to a dry-goods shop. The boy first introduced himself as Raju and then presented me to the shopkeepers, his mother and father. The Nepali word saahuji, which was widely used in carpet factories to describe those in charge, is actually more appropriately used to describe shopkeepers such as Raju's parents. Shopkeepers, particularly in Nepal's hill and mountain regions, are among of the few people consistently engaged with the cash economy, as they trade in goods and provide credit services for poor villagers, often imposing usurious rates of credit (Zivetz 1992).

Raju's father opened a miniature refrigerator and cracked the cap off of a cold bottle of orange drink. He handed it to me with a smile, refusing the 10 rupee note I held out to him. Raju then led me to his room, where I sat on his bed surrounded by posters of Hindi film heroes and fluffy white kittens with captions of inspirational thought. Raju told me that he was a student, waiting to take his passing-out SLC examination, which allowed Nepalese students to apply to any one of the growing number of private "campuses" that would, in turn, permit application to university. Raju told me that he wanted to study commerce in America. I looked out the window towards the factory and saw the usual collection of youths loitering and smoking cigarettes: no saahuji, no Dorje, though I likely wouldn't recognize him even if he were there. Raju was still talking, and as was the case with most Nepali youths I talked to, the topic turned to politics. Raju, like his parents, was a dedicated Congress Party supporter. He began to relay the tribulations of BP Koirala, who had been deposed and imprisoned by the present king's father. Raju railed against the king and his supporters: "they will destroy the nation," he said, and continued on with a passionate, though now for me, tired narrative. I did not want to spend my morning sipping soft drinks under posters of a beefy Sanjay Dutt, listening to this boy's heartfelt convictions and dreams. Where was Dorje Lama?

Finally, Raju rose, looked out the window and pulled me up, "he is there," he said, and we raced down the steps to catch him. At the door to the factory he called into the room, and a red-eyed youth, apparently no older than the weavers still seated at their looms, came forward. Other faces followed, glaring at us from inside the dark weaving hall. Raju spoke rapidly to the youth, but before I could make out what was said, the youth muttered a reply, turned on his heel, and went back inside. The other faces remained at the door, looking suspicious and menacing. Raju looked sheepishly at me. "He has declined our request for an interview," he reported.

"What? Isn't this Dorje Lama? He telephoned me last night and invited me to come here!" The faces in the door swivelled in vague, figure-eight patterns, then disappeared back inside. Confused and a little frustrated, I gave Raju my card and a promise to get in touch with him another time and went home. I had wasted a whole morning waiting to meet the wrong person.

That night the telephone rang again. It was Dorje. "Where were you?" he demanded. I explained how I'd become lost and described my encounter with the people at the other factory. Dorje thought for a moment. "That is a very bad place," he reflected and then suggested, "Tomorrow we can meet at the stupa gate and I will take you to my factory."

The next day Dorje met me promptly at the stupa gate and led me back to his house, not far from the factory that I had blundered into the previous day. As his wife served tea and his children prepared for school, it occurred to me how unusual this was. For weeks I had been struggling to meet and interview people in the carpet industry, only to be disappointed by missed appointments and evasive or dismissive discussions. Dorje had sought me out, guided me to his home, and wanted to talk. Clearly he had a voice and wished to be heard. I was still unclear about, and even a little suspicious of, why he was making such an effort. I understood my objectives in building a relationship with him, but surely he had his own. Dorje Lama told me that he hired workers who had been fired from other factories, as such was the lot of a small-scale saahuji who did not have the resources to pay the higher piece rates offered by the owners of larger or more established enterprises. Over the several months that I visited his home cum factory, there was an even larger turnover of weavers than anywhere else. Dorje was often torn between searching for subcontracts to weave and weavers to weave them. Often there was no work and, when there was work, there was often no one to do it. The first time Dorje invited me to see his weaving shed, located in the front yard of his rented compound, I was shocked to find about a dozen very young children sitting on planks, tiny hands rapidly assaulting the warps of their loom. Dorje beamed as he unrolled a completed carpet for my approval. I said it was fine, but was unable to tear my eyes away from the gaze of the young boys at work, who stared back at me. Dorje introduced me to an older boy sitting at one end of the row – he was their *thekadaar* (labour contractor). I sat down beside him and talked about the carpets they were weaving as Dorje excused himself and returned upstairs. I was gripped by visceral horror. I admired Dorje and had grown to like him. Now here he was, an exploiter of young children, technically a criminal and an object of international condemnation. After a few minutes, I excused myself and dashed into the alley without even saying goodbye.

After about a week I summoned enough courage to return. Child labour was, after all, a major factor in my work. As I entered the rusted iron door of the compound, Dorje leapt from the door of his weaving shed and grasped my hand: "Where were you?" I muttered something about not feeling well. Dorje took me by the hand and led me back into the weaving shed. The boys and their thekadaar were gone; in their place were four teenagers, a boy and three girls, who giggled when they saw me. "Where did your other weavers go?" I asked. "They had to go back to school," Dorje lamented. I knew that there had been a national school holiday the previous week, because the roads and pathways had been jammed with children at play. Now they were gone and the monotonous sound of school children chanting their studies was once again part of the street soundscape. Dorje's explanation was plausible and I never again saw weavers as young as those I had previously seen working at his looms.

On my next visit, Dorje was not around. The four young weavers who worked with him at the time told me that he was out, perhaps searching for carpet orders, wool, or weavers, preparing for puja, or just visiting, though, in practice, all of those tasks could have been combined in a single journey. These weavers, who appeared to be in their late teens, were not working when I arrived, but rather were lounging in Dorje's living room drinking tea. The boundary between home and factory, economic production and domesticity, which was blurred in most of the small factories I visited, was even more so in Dorje's place. These young weavers came and went from their boss's living area at their whim. I often found the oldest of them, a twenty-year old woman who served informally as a carpet master for Dorje, chatting and gossiping with his wife as she brewed salt tea. Both would tease me in the Yolmo language and, when I asked for a translation, they giggled uncontrollably and refused to comply.

Now things were slow, they said, as there was nothing to weave. This led me to speculate that Dorje was out visiting exporters and other subcontractors looking for carpet orders. He had told me that I was welcome anytime, even if he wasn't there, so when the four weavers invited me to have tea, I took the opportunity to speak with them about their lives and their work. I had with me a camera, as Dorje had consented to my taking photographs in his factory for study purposes. One of the girls noticed the camera and asked if I would take her picture. As she ran to her room to put on a costume more fitting than the dusty skirt she was wearing, two of the other weavers dove into a trunk that contained Dorje's wife's clothing and began to model different combinations. When something struck their fancy, they ran across the hall to change into it. I spent a couple of hours photographing them in the bright afternoon light that flooded into the room, all under the watchful eyes of Guru Rinpoche who peered down from a colourful *thangka* (religious painting) in Dorje's cabinet.

One of the girls retrieved a gold wristwatch from the chest and held it across her chest as I snapped a shot, then passed it to the others so that they could also wear it when their photos were taken. At another point, the only male in the group ran to his room and returned with a T-shirt that depicted the macabre album cover of an American heavy metal band – the red-eyed face of a corpse that bore some resemblance to the three demon heads that were impaled on the Guru's staff in the *thangka*. I had often seen these T-shirts for sale in the local markets and noticed that they were extremely popular among young males. This time, each of the weavers took a turn wearing the shirt. It was a prized possession, something to be seen in, even though it was likely offloaded onto the South Asian market as a cheap and somewhat worthless commodity that could not be sold elsewhere. At first I tried to use the occasion to learn more about the economics of weaving labour, but quickly abandoned this approach to focus on the aesthetics of the experience. Two rolls of expensive Ektachrome film, obtained with difficulty, which I had intended to use on carpet looms, were expended instead on this scene. I told the young weavers that I would process the film and bring some slides to them the following week.

When I arrived the next week, Dorje still had not returned, and three of the four weavers were no longer there, as they had moved on to find work elsewhere. Only the carpet master remained, as she was also responsible for caring for the house while Dorje was away. I presented her with copies of the slides that I had taken and she promised to somehow distribute them to the others. She looked at a portrait of herself wearing a graceful blue traditional dress with a striking jade necklace and earrings and the bright gold wristwatch on her arm. Dressed as such in dramatic light she looked mature, beautiful, and poised, not the waif-like girl she appeared to be at her loom. However, she turned up her nose: "I look fat," she said. I tried to disagree, but she would not be convinced. This obsession with weight and appearance reminded me of adolescents I knew at home. She was young and needed to look her best.

In the course of my initial research on the carpet industry I came across an article written by Thomas Guta (1992) in a trade magazine, which helpfully described the "cutting loops" method that distinguished Tibetan carpet weaving from other oriental weaving traditions (see also Denwood 1974). Thomas Guta was another stranger in this place, an American artist who was drawn here because of his passion for handmade carpets and his admiration, in particular, for the Tibetan weaving tradition. He was also a designer, who drew upon Tibetan motifs to create his own carpets, and a writer who somewhat romantically promoted the carpet as a handmade craft that connected the weaver to the Tibetan tradition. I don't know if his observations of Boudhanath were different from my own, as I never met him, even though he certainly would have walked the same roads and paths that I was mapping. He died in a tragic air accident in 1992, before the controversies about child labour in the industry erupted a year later (CWIN 1992).

In that article there appears an eloquent paragraph that framed and in some ways haunted my fieldwork throughout the year I lived there:

> The finished rug wasn't the end. Once it was trimmed, sheared and cut from the loom, they strung it up again. Weaving was well practiced, the rug, well used. Carpets wore from the centre out, and were replaced like their very clothing, by putting another over or under the worn piece, depending on the occasion. The rugs were worn down to a pileless sheen. The final tribute to their craft was that almost nothing survived. What survived was the practice of hitching, tying off and cutting through. In it, they grounded their vision, and perfected their view. In the space of one knot swooping down over the bar, they listened to wisdom's descent. It rolled off their looms, sailed out of the doorways to mesh with life's great tangle. (Guta 1992, 68)

Guta's account of the weaving process, of course, ignores its more oppressive aspects. Many of the weavers I observed were not grounding their labour in any vision: they were being ground down by long hours, low pay, and usurious wage credit practices (O'Neill 2004). The authenticity of their product, moreover, was to be questioned, for beyond the continued use of the "cutting loops" method, carpets were woven on industrial looms with chemically dyed wool, based on patterns faxed in from designers in Germany, Switzerland, and the USA. But Guta's romanticism appeals to me, in spite of its ignorance of working conditions and the globalized structure of the industry, because it describes for me the aspiration that people like Dorje and his weavers had invested in what was for them both a new craft and an opportunity to mesh with the modern world. And Boudhanath, whose tangled traditional footpaths now were being paved and fixed into that world, was the stage for these aspirations.

As the fieldwork wore on, my wanderings through Boudhanath, though intentional, became more and more open to ends that were suggested by the streets and footpaths themselves. The past that we moderns were attempting to commodify and move beyond was much more resilient than many of theorists I read suggested. Boudhanath seemed to confound attempts to consume it; roads led to empty fields and disappeared, footpaths twisted between the tenements and ended at brick walls, as if their makers were similarly distracted. Gradually, as I walked systematically over what was to be my research area, I began to notice elements of this tradition, sometimes fading, sometimes bold, but always invigorated by change.

It is impossible for a map to express the phenomenology of being in a place or to inscribe what was present before and how its past struggles with its future. A map is little more than a snapshot of changing relationships, frozen in time. Mapping Boudhanath was not only a way to know and control space, it was also a way of insinuating my place within it. Boudhanath has always been an ambiguous place where, for centuries, many different peoples had come as monks, pilgrims, migrants, tourists, weavers, and researchers. By drawing a map by foot, eye, and pen I fixed my place within Boudhanath's tangle.

Chapter Four

You Should Not Be Too Big a Person

We share Nepal with the dogs. Thousands of them, howling, almost human. By day, they twist into one another in the hot sun, then sleep. At night, they guard red meat under butcher stalls, stake out territory. Reach for a rock, they will let you pass. Walking home one night, we hear both the occasional crescendo of a distant folksong and the dogs. The music is reassuring. A group of men approach us, keeping the dogs at bay as they near. "*Tom-ji*," one calls out. It is Dorje Lama, descending the road towards us. We are relieved to strike up the local greeting:

"Where have you been?"
"Oh, here and there."
"Where are you going now?"
"Home."

Dorje casts a stone into the darkness. A dog whimpers and scuttles back across the road to cower in a ditch. He takes my hand and points over to a red glow rising from a compound nearby. "It is a Sherpa festival," he says. "Please come." We are ushered inside, where two lines of men and women face each other over the fire, their voices rising and falling in Yolmo dialect. I cannot understand what is being said, but the form of the songs reminds me of something that I had read while preparing my literature review. What was the author's name? What was that book?

We are directed to sit. I see many familiar faces – people I have recently interviewed, people I chat with every day, purchase soft drinks and newspapers from, or just seem to recognize from the bazaars and temples of the neighbourhood. I identify Nechung Lama and his family sitting on a blanket, as glasses of hot raksi are pressed into our hands. He smiles back, and it suddenly occurs to me what the name of the book was, and that the author was describing a cycle of funerary songs that are relayed from men to women. I remembered that the piece struck me as poignantly showing music as a powerful medium that, for many of us, allows an exploration of grief, loss, and our own mortality. My thesis was not about death or music, however, and the memory of reading that book was so submerged that it failed to provide much help in understanding what I was hearing and seeing.

Yet if this is a funeral, it is not like any that I have ever attended. People are laughing, drinking, and singing. Nechung's daughter is trying to learn English and she pulls my wife aside to practise. I am suddenly aware that men are sitting with men and women with women. Across the fire, the two lines continue to trade verses. Nechung pushes me to my feet and Dorje drags me into the line with the other men to dance across the flame.

I study my feet, and then theirs. The choreography is deceptively simple, appearing to be a hop followed by two stamps of the right foot followed by a sweeping kick forward, repeated to the rhythm of the music. Still, I cannot master it and I finally allow the two men holding me in the line to swing me back and forth like a rag doll. There is good-natured laughter around me, and even the women point across the fire and smile broadly. The song ends and people I have never met come up and compliment my efforts. The dancers return to their families, to their reveries.

At the end of what is left of the line, I see a man weeping openly. Tears stream down his face as several other men embrace him in consolation. I realize then that this is a funeral and that I am observing a deeply personal moment of grief. I understand too that I am the stranger present. Later, as we head home, keeping to one side to avoid confronting the dogs, I think of the dancing, the singing, and the tears, and I wonder where and how do I fit in this space? Before sleep I write a note in my field journal, describing in bare detail the events in which I had just participated. I am the observer. I am the outsider. The words seem only to untangle my experience of the events.

I met Dorje again after he had returned from Uttar Bhanyang the following week. As I suspected, he had been there to find weavers to work on orders he had obtained from an exporter. Unfortunately, he had arrived in Uttar Bhanjyang too late; he told me that another labour contractor had already been there and hired every available person for work in a different factory. When they are not employed, many weavers go back to their villages to attend to their land and other family affairs, returning to the city to work when they are collected by a thekadaar or saahuji. Many of the young people in Uttar Bhanjyang were skilled weavers and Dorje had hoped to hire some of them to fulfil his contract. Now he had a dilemma: he had too few weavers on hand to get the contract completed on time, but he could not surrender the contract uncompleted, as that would destroy his reputation in the industry. Since hundreds of small-scale subcontractors were competing for fewer and fewer contracts, his export patron would merely turn to a more established and trustworthy saahuji. Dorje may have had to wait a long time for his next chance of finding a lucrative patron, a chance that might never materialize.

I found Dorje one afternoon by chance as I was visiting another small factory run by two brothers, Mingmar and Tsering, to ask them some additional questions. All of them were from Uttar Bhanjyang – their homes faced each other across Dorje's father's millet field – and they frequently cooperated with each other in their small-scale enterprises in Boudhanath. Mingmar and Tsering had a factory full of weavers, many of them children, and had been subsisting by weaving cheap stock carpets, which forced them to pay out a low piece rate. They agreed to take the bulk of Dorje's order on a sub-subcontract basis, for which they would be paid a higher "program" rate (although they did not increase their weaver's rate), and Dorje would be able to protect his reputation with his patron.

Though Dorje, Mingmar, and Tsering were collaborators in this arrangement, which could not be revealed to the exporter commissioning the carpets, they were also competitors as small-scale, autonomous saahuji. After all, Mingmar and Tsering also were searching for program orders and trying to find more lucrative work, so Dorje's collaboration with them as fellow villagers was risky. I knew Mingmar and Tsering to be shrewd, seasoned saahuji, even though they, like Dorje, were young men. Where Dorje had grown up in Uttar Bhanjyang and had migrated to Boudhanath only a few years earlier, the brothers had been collected by a thekadaar many years earlier and had grown up in carpet factories. They knew the business from the warp and weft up and were wise to the intricacies of the trade. Dorje was nevertheless relieved to be able to salvage his position.

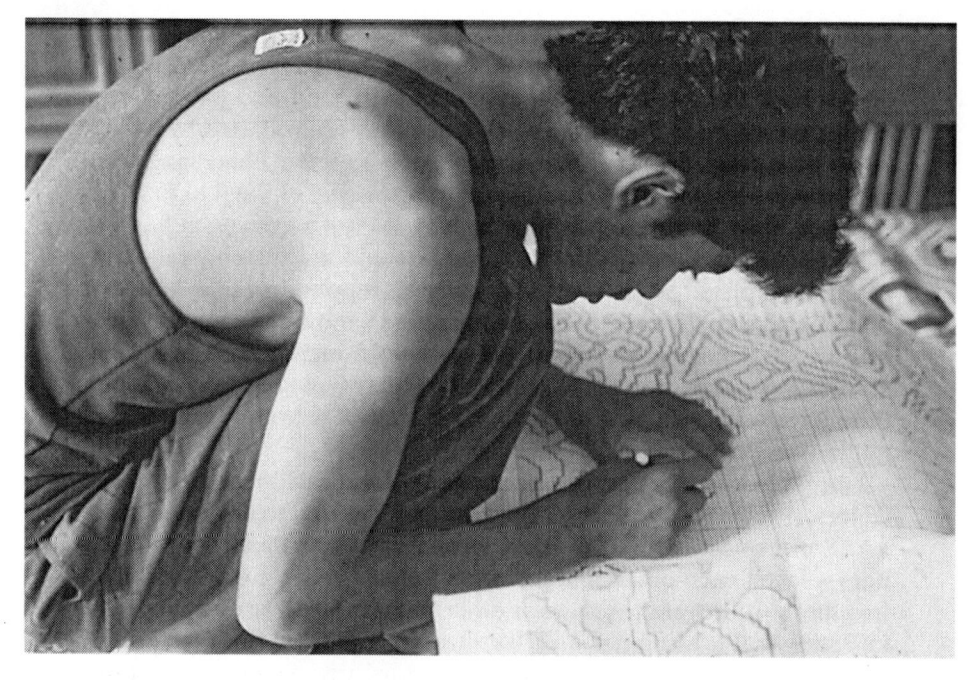

Figure 4.1. A graphic artist traces a carpet design on full-size graph paper, to be attached to the loom for weaving, March 1995.

The four of us sat in Mingmar and Tsering's spartan quarters, chatting as an employee huddled over a makeshift light table and sketched one of the program designs on graph paper. In the hallway, an elderly woman dressed in an ash-covered dress spun wool from a loose pile on the floor into tight, perfectly round balls. Tsering began playing a recording of Yolmo songs for me on a battered tape recorder, but quickly tired of the music and slipped the tape back into its case, substituting one of popular Nepali songs. There was a knock on the door, and another man appeared and entered into a heated exchange with Mingmar. The conversation, in Nepali, was too rapid for me to follow and in any case I was uncomfortable being in the middle of their debate, so I strained to listen to the Nepali music in which a high-pitched chanteuse lamented a lost love.

Mingmar switched to Yolmo and appeared to summon the elderly woman in the hallway, who rose and, glaring at the intruding man, produced a key from behind her apron. Mingmar took it, unlocked the metal strongbox in the corner of the room, and produced a wad of rupees that the intruder grabbed. The elderly woman berated him in Nepali as he retreated to the stairs, then turned to Mingmar, switched to Yolmo, and began scolding him as well. Mingmar sheepishly handed the key back to the woman, who I then realized was his mother and evidently held considerable power over the conduct of the business. She sat down to continue spooling, Mingmar resumed smoking his cheroot, and the rest of us strained our ears to the music to avoid any further conflict.

Dorje stood up to leave and I joined him, as I felt an awkward tension in the room. Tsering shot up with us: "Where are you going?" I had some additional questions to ask, but knew that this was not a good time to ask them, so I said that I could come back later in the week if they would be available. Mingmar seemed confused: "But you already asked your questions." I explained that I wanted to understand more. Their mother was now glaring at me. Nervous, I blurted out that I wanted to know more from them because I was becoming more interested in the plight of small-scale producers like himself. On reflection, this was an honest response, as I found myself more and more caught up with the affairs of Dorje and of Mingmar and Tsering, in part because they were from Helambu, a place I was familiar with and where I had connections, but also in part because it was they who were attempting to move a greater social distance than anyone else in the industry. While most exporters were second-generation Tibetan refugees, well educated in elite private schools and able to sustain the sympathies of their Western partners in English (and German), the young men from Helambu had risen in a very short time from the status of peasants and bearers of loads (Campbell 1997) to near middle-class status as petty capitalists. If globalization were to have any value, I thought, it should make a significant difference for these people.

Mingmar and Tsering looked at each other as if in consultation. Tsering then said, "There is someone you should meet. He is one of our own people." The two brothers led us outside, down a dusty pathway between tenements, past an annoyed water buffalo that strained at its tether as if wanting to attack, to a nearby building. They tapped on a door, it opened, and they introduced me to Nechung Lama.

The men (and, occasionally, women) that I wanted to work with were entrepreneurs, people like Dorje who had sufficient capital in all of its forms to try to profit from the explosion of Tibetan carpet exports since 1989. A few of them were profiting handsomely from the carpets, some of them were making a modest living, and many were struggling to survive what seemed a calamity of rapid change, a transforming field on which they were unsure and perhaps ill equipped to compete. Having material wealth alone was no sure way to make it. A person needed connections – social networks, as we like to say – and plenty of the right kind of knowledge that could be useful later on. People in Boudhanath referred to this network as *aaphno maanchhe* (our own people), signifying the network of friends, family, and convenient acquaintances that enabled them to survive and even flourish. Aaphno maanchhe implied many varieties of relationships: marriage, jati, affiliation, kinship (sanguineal, consanguineal, and fictive), education (or lack of it), affective or merely tolerant.

Even though the industry served as a means of raising the social status and affluence of many in the Tibetan and Tibetan co-religionist communities, it was also dangerous, as it required new associations with people across problematic social boundaries. Aaphno maanchhe played an important role in building trust among carpet exporters, subcontractors, thekadaar, and weavers, because aaphno maanchhe produced what Anthony Giddens (1990) calls the "facework trust" of a traditional social order. In such an order social identity structures knowledge about whom one could do business with. In a transnational industry that brought people of many classes, castes, and knowledge levels together in an antagonistic field governed by competition and limited resources, aaphno maanchhe was no longer sufficient to build trust. What was required were abstract forms of trust – law, contracts – that assured actors that agreements would be honoured and that people could be held accountable for their actions. The primordial solidarity that seems to follow from networks of "our own people" may build trust for traditional forms of economic collaboration, but the size, scope, and complexity of the carpet industry revealed the limitations of traditional networks. What was required was not mere familiarity, but the trust, according to Barbara Misztal (1996, 50),"that lies between absolute knowledge and absolute ignorance – when one cannot assess probabilities."

Small-scale saahuji faced the real possibility that they could fail, and no relationship could be a guarantee against it. Many of them were unaware of the global economic and social influences on their livelihoods, such as rising and falling consumer demand in Europe, price fixing by profit-hungry carpet importers and exporters, international anti-child labour campaigns, and threatened boycotts. They also faced local uncertainties: whether they would be beaten out of a lucrative subcontract by another competitor, or would not be able to obtain trained weavers in a timely fashion, or would be cheated by another thekadaar or saahuji. But the news that traditional social networks were irrelevant to modern economic life had not really reached many of the carpet entrepreneurs that I interviewed. For them, aaphno maanchhe continued to be the preferred way of managing productive relations, under the assumption that anyone who fell into that category would act predictably and reliably. The notion that someone from within that group would act in strategic self-interest seemed, on the surface at least, unthinkable. Though they wanted to succeed, they did not see taking advantage of another within that group as a legitimate means of success, even though, all too often, circumstances rewarded self-interest over other considerations.

What I was to discover was that my observing these networks, my point of view on their point of view, implicated me as an active member in this community of people as they flourished or failed in the new economy of Boudhanath. I was a part of their aaphno maanchhe; it was not possible to work with them otherwise.

In contrast to Mingmar and Tsering's manufactory, Nechung Lama's factory was bustling with activity. There were only twelve upright looms in the cramped weaving hall, but both sides of each were dressed and being operated by young weavers. Several of the women were nursing babies at their seats, and a makeshift cradle nestling another sleeping infant was tied precariously between two of the loom rails. On each loom an almost identical carpet was taking form, a cobalt blue open field framed by an abstract, pastel coloured border. They looked nothing like the traditional Tibetan carpets featured in industry publications or that were seen hanging in front of the tourist curio shops that ring the Boudhanath stupa. They were, however, the industry-standard, European-design carpets that were being mass produced for the world market. Nechung's manufactory looked comparatively prosperous – the order sheets that I saw attached to each loom bore the letterhead of a prominent Tibetan export firm.

The three-storey brick building his manufactory occupied was, like many new buildings, dark and bare; concrete steps littered with bits of loose wool led upstairs from the weaving room to the weavers' quarters. Several of them were upstairs as we went by, attending to a whistling pressure cooker on a propane stove. Nechung led us into his large but austere living room, and we sat down on the single bed that served as a sofa.

He called a young boy into the room, passed him a wad of rupee notes and sent him out for refreshments. A woman wearing a dusty brown *bhaku* came in with flask of sweet tea. Mingmar and Tsering began speaking about how difficult business was – for Mingmar there were no orders, he was weaving only models and for stock (he did not mention the orders he had just obtained from Dorje), while Nechung complained about the price of wool. The boy returned with three lukewarm bottles of syrupy orange soda and a package of "Yak" brand cigarettes, which appeared to contain chunks of yak wool along with stale tobacco.

The long, rambling conversation we had that day in Nechung's room was unrecorded – even the few notes I made are brief and undetailed – yet it shaped the outcome of my research project more fundamentally than almost any other. Mingmar, Dorje, and Nechung were what many

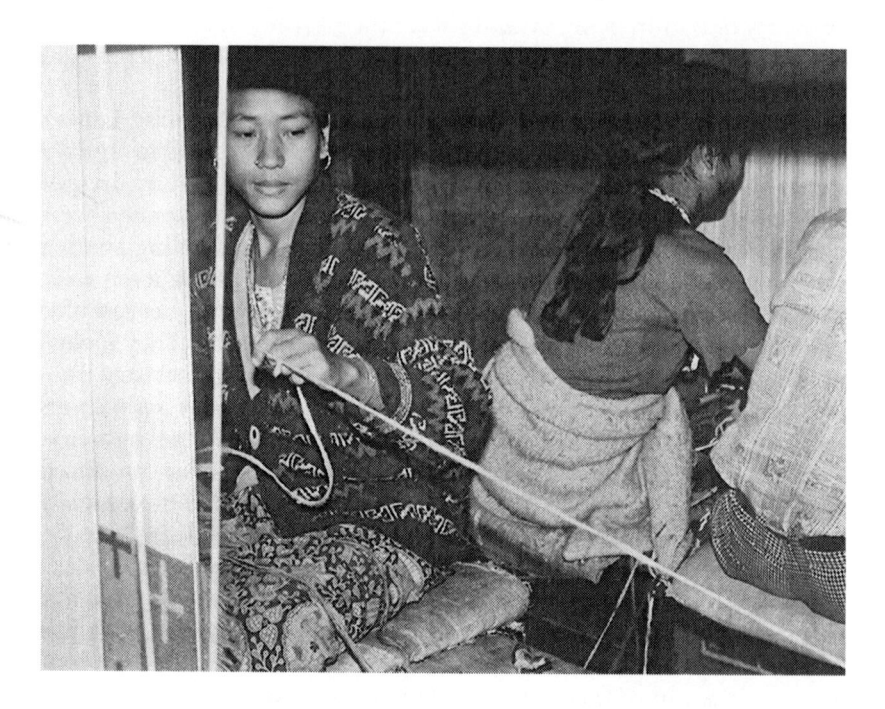

Figure 4.2. Carpet weaver, Jorpati VDC, November 1998.

anthropologists described as "petty capitalists," a term borrowed from the neo-Marxist literature that was predominant in the study of small-scale capitalism in the 1970s. The term itself is misleading, as it appears to belittle a class of limited, autonomous enterprises that play an important role both in developing economies and, increasingly, in the era of "flexible accumulation" that characterizes the postmodern economy (Harvey 1989; see also Smart and Smart 2005). The Tibetan refugee exporters of Boudhanath/Jorpati needed small carpet manufactories, such as Nechung's, to subcontract work, thus avoiding expensive and risky investments in their own infrastructure (more looms means more space, more weaving labour, and more management staff).

The crux of the neo-Marxist argument is that small-scale, or petty, producers like Nechung are subordinated to more powerful capital interests to the extent that their work is little more than disguised wage labour, and that whatever autonomy or flexibility they may think they have is illusory or, at the very least, subject to the capriciousness of the market. This illusion of autonomy epitomizes the epistemological distinction that Marx made between "men in the flesh" and men as they narrate themselves, and the broader ontological distinction between human nature and alienated consciousness. These theories raced through my mind as I sipped the soda and drew on the stale cigarette, listening to Nechung and Tsering complaining about the sudden, precipitous increase in wool prices that ate through their already paper-thin profit margins. I could not reconcile neo-Marxist theory with this experience of bearing risk, at least not so long as I shared in their meagre luxuries.

As we talked, curious people spilled into the room. There were children, some without trousers or shorts, obviating the need for diapers, and some of the older ones were dressed in blue school uniforms with the name of the school embroidered on their breast pockets. Young women and men were whispering, studying me, giggling at my awkward Nepali. After weeks of false starts, unproductive meetings, and hours wasted in the waiting rooms of large export factories, my meeting with Mingmar, Tsering, and Nechung that day seemed my first authentic contact with the folk who made carpets. The conversation, however, was mostly between the carpet saahuji, and I strained to understand what was being said. Mingmar noticed and summed it up for me: "*Aajaa bholi carpet ekdom garho chha*" (These days the carpet business is very hard). Wool prices had almost doubled in a few short months, and everyone agreed that this was because the Madhesi who controlled the import of New Zealand wool held a monopoly on supply. Shyam later told me that the use of Madhesi in this context was unusual, as it generally was taken to refer to the ethnically distinct lowland people of Nepal and North India, but not to the Marwari merchant caste that was rumoured to control wool supplies. This discourse of ethnic and caste hierarchy permeated everyday conversation, but the precise structure of that hierarchy was elusive; it appeared different from each perspective I encountered. What was shared was a sense that caste or ethnic identity was of signal importance in knowing whom one could trust or who was on one's side.

Our conversation turned from business to talk of their village in Helambu. We learned that we shared acquaintance with many people from there, as all three men were lamas from Uttar Bhanjyang, which is one of the temple villages described in Clarke's "Helambu History" (1980) and which I also recognized as one I had passed through four years earlier on my way to Yangrima. Nechung invited me to return, showing me how his name was spelled on a receipt from the Tibetan company to which he supplied carpets on subcontract. Cued by this observation, I asked them if they had ever thought of exporting carpets themselves, as I was interested in learning about the cultural and material barriers they faced in expanding their enterprises. They told me that they needed to produce at least 1,500 metres of carpet every month for export and/or have a large sum of foreign currency in the bank. They then suggested that I could open a factory in Canada. We all laughed, but I was unsure about whether the irony of the joke was shared in equal measure.

I was eager to interview Nechung, as he appeared to have a grounded perspective on the carpet industry and also, unlike many of the other men I had met, shared his experience with alacrity. On my next visit, I arrived with Shyam at an arranged time with the standard list of questions I had written for all of the producers we spoke with and the tape recorder loaded with a fresh cassette tape. Nechung's two sons had just finished their pre-school meal and were packing up for the schoolday. One of them had spilled some of his dal bhaat on the carpet and Nechung was apologetically sweeping it up. I entered and sat down as I was directed, but Shyam remained sullenly at the door until the food was cleared away. Despite this initial apprehension, he settled in and struck a familiar chord with Nechung as we began to discuss the letter of consent that I needed him to sign. I explained this to Nechung first, outlining its basic terms and reassuring him that its intent was to protect his confidentiality. Nechung looked perplexed, so I reiterated what I had just said, growing inwardly more uneasy about his response. Nechung gave no response, so we both looked to Shyam for assistance. He again went over the content of the letter in some detail, assuring Nechung that I had to get his signature before we could begin the interview. Nechung then pressed his palms together, slightly inclined his head, and then told us that he did not want to sign the letter. My inward unease turned to panic. I asked Nechung if he no longer wanted to do the interview; he told us that he did, that we could ask our questions and record. "But," Shyam said, "you will need to sign the letter first, so that you will know to trust us." Again, Nechung refused.

This was unknown territory for me, as it was not a refusal to participate in the research as several people had already done. That would have been understandable, as many carpet producers were busy people, and researchers and journalists had given them good reason not to speak with outsiders. Nechung's refusal pertained only to signing the letter, not to the interview, and this situation had never been anticipated in the well-intentioned education on the ethics of doing research that I had received as a graduate student. Shyam asked Nechung why he would not sign the letter. Nechung looked at me, then back at Shyam, and explained, "He is like our own people (aaphno maanchhe), so we don't need a letter to trust each other." How he could have made such a determination after only one meeting, I didn't know, but his response deepened the dilemma we found ourselves in: do we continue or politely decline to do the interview?

Fieldwork, at least the fieldwork that we conducted in teeming and transient peri-urban Kathmandu, often entailed this kind of decision that had to be made in the moment. Sometimes it led to happy accidents and sometimes to mistakes that ended up wasting time and energy. At that moment, I decided to go ahead with the interview, even though recording it was contrary to the conditions of my funding and to the fetishistic obsession of my institutional review board with "informed consent." Because of that decision, my work with Nechung – which would proceed regularly for the next six months of fieldwork and the next ten years (and counting) of our lives – has never rested comfortably in the prescribed categories of social science or, rather, in the scientific genres of human understanding. The subjection of Nechung and his life to theoretical categories of comparative ethnography was a necessary part of my own career path after leaving the field. This is what my discipline, my colleagues, and perhaps even the reader expects of ethnography.

Nechung's refusal to sign that letter that day, and my decision to proceed regardless, marked our collaboration as one based on facework trust, not the legitimated confidence of a written code. Therefore, the analysis of his entrepreneurial activity for comparative study ran the risk of violating that trust.

Nechung's reference to me as "aaphno maanchhe" struck me as possibly disingenuous and perhaps opportunistic. To that point I had understood the term as described by the Nepalese anthropologist Dor Bahadur Bista (1991, 89): a social network through which individuals advanced their own interests and raised their status. In Bista's view, these networks were central to the way Nepal was governed by its Brahmin and Chetris elites, and they thwarted the meritocracy that he argued was necessary for Nepal's modernization. Aaphno maanchhe could be understood as a small-scale trust network, often based on but not confined to ethnic, caste, or regional affiliation. Nechung's immediate network was made up almost entirely of people from Uttar Bhanjyang, people with whom he shared information, equivalent subcontracts, labour, and materials. It was what his success was based on. Unlike legitimated forms of confidence, such as those provided by contract and other laws, the interpersonal trust that aaphno maanchhe exploits is subject to abuse by individuals who pursue their own self-interest too closely. I learned the following week that Mingmar had taken advantage of our visit with Nechung to filch a carpet design from his factory. Nechung told me he was no longer on speaking terms with Mingmar when he discovered that he was producing suspiciously similar carpets for stock sales. These designs are proprietary, and the exporters who own them are particularly concerned that they do not fall into the hands of stock weavers, who could undervalue their own orders with cheaper carpets. Their falling-out was short lived, however, as I saw them later participating together in a local religious ceremony, collaborating in their ritual obligations as if nothing had happened.

Now that I was a member of this social network, I wondered about the possible implications. In an insightful essay on the social functions of trust and confidence, Niklas Luhmann (1988, 97) argues that trust in interpersonal relations is insufficient for modern, complex economies, divisions of labour, and politics; that confidence in institutions must assure predictability and obviate the need to make risky choices, because "if you choose one action in preference to others in spite of being disappointed by the activities of others, you define the situation as one of trust." The implication is that institutional confidence will produce assurances that outcomes will be predictable, whereas interpersonal trust in social networks, as the falling-out between Nechung and Mingmar showed, is risky, particularly when social, economic, and political rules are being rewritten in a period of expansive change. I could not know then what twists and turns my collaboration with Nechung would take, but I accepted his invitation to undertake it.

My visits with Nechung became more frequent as the fieldwork continued, since I found that he could answer many of the questions raised in other interviews or through other observations, particularly on the risks that small-scale entrepreneurs bore in the volatile carpet market. On one afternoon, we spent a long time discussing carpet piece rates, a complicated and sometimes technical topic that was nevertheless important for me to master in order to evaluate the many different claims about them that I was collecting in my data. Despite his lack of education, Nechung had a comprehensive understanding of the carpet market that extended far beyond his own workshop. He told me, for example, that for each square metre shipped abroad, carpet exporters were paid a government regulated "export price" by European or American carpet importers, imposed to ensure that foreign currency was paid into and stayed in Nepal. Despite this policy, there was a widespread custom among importers of sending the export rate for their purchases, even though, in reality, they were paying less to Nepalese exporters. Nepalese exporters would then remit the difference to the importer – a practice that enriched European carpet importers with tax-free earnings. This procedure was illegal, as it meant that there was less foreign currency in the country than was accounted for and therefore there was less money to pay wages or benefits to workers. But the practice was widely known to most inside the industry, Nechung included. So much for Luhmann's "confidences" in global markets – it cheated the very people whose hands lent the Tibetan carpet its handmade reputation.

Nechung and I sat at his desk and punched numbers into his calculator, noting how much for wool, labour, carpet washing, conveyance to the exporter's warehouse, rent of the factory building, and motorcycle operation and maintenance. We tried out different permutations, changing variables and situations. I began to understand from our math that many producers and weavers were giving me wildly erratic data, exaggerated labour costs, underestimated profit margins, and inflated productivity reports.

As was usually the case, the dusty office room where we did our calculations was full of onlookers, mostly young men who peered over our shoulders and made frequent comments. Nechung consulted them for their views, sometimes in Nepali, at other times in the Yolmo dialect, and they responded, correcting labour costs, petrol prices, and the time it took to weave carpets. When we had all but exhausted the subject of piece rates, one of the youths asked me, "How much money do you make?" They had turned the tables on me and waited with their fingers at the calculator to analyse my answers. "Where?" I asked for clarification; "Here, or in Canada?" "In Nepal." At first I was reluctant to answer, but then reasoned that I had just spent the last hour asking Nechung about *his* finances. I divided my grant budget into months and gave them an approximate figure. "American dollars?" "No, Canadian; about 36 rupees to the dollar." Fingers tapped rapidly at the calculator, a sum appeared on the grey screen, and it was passed among the men. There were several whistles and guffaws of amazement. I hastily objected that from that sum had to come the rental for my flat, the salary for three research assistants, supplies, but they appeared disinterested in my explanation. "And in Canada how much?" Again, I approximated by adding my scholarship to my salary as a university teaching assistant, dividing by 12. More tapping at the calculator, more whistles. Again, I qualified my answer with the example that it cost $2.50 CAD to take a bus to the campus where I worked, which was equivalent to 90 rupees. By contrast, a taxi from Boudhanath to Durbar Marg in Kathmandu was 30 rupees if you bargained hard, a tempo ride was 6 rupees and an overcrowded bus ride was 2 rupees and 50 paise. One of them briefly acknowledged my explanation while the men stared at the figure on the calculator screen, talking excitedly among themselves about what that money could purchase in Nepal – a small automobile or the down payment on a house. I had failed to put these figures into context for them. Nechung shooed them from the wool room and told them to get back to work or else they wouldn't even see their own salary.

This counter-interrogation was an almost daily feature of the research I did in 1995, as well as of the dialogue that I continued to conduct with people in Nepal ten years later. Their subjecting me to comparative economic analysis belies the fictive construction of the passive fieldwork "informant" as an object of ethnographic study. They are clearly as interested in me – my culture, practices, and beliefs –as I am in them. Perhaps even more so: their enumerations reflect a calculated curiosity, a sizing up or evaluation of our respective positions in the world. They reminded me, and continue to remind me, of the inequality between our worlds, of the disproportionate distribution of wealth, of resources, and more important here, of living potential, which characterizes the modern global system. This is a disparity on which they continually remark.

On the face of it Nechung Lama's potential was, at that point, fairly strong. He was receiving regular subcontracts from one of the largest exporters in Nepal and enjoyed a solid reputation among other carpet producers as a competent carpet maker. His factory was modest, but working at full capacity, and though he shared living space with his workers, his own apartments were comparatively comfortable. He paid substantial fees for two of his sons to attend a private English school, which gave them an education that many people believed was superior to that of the local government schools. Another son was supported as a Buddhist monk at a monastery in India, thus making an important contribution to his religion and earning merit for himself and his community. Nechung appeared to be one of the most successful saahuji around, a master carpet weaver and an important man among the people from Uttar Bhanjyang. Yet he never spoke immodestly about his achievements, choosing rather to narrate a communal ethos of social equality – "*Thulo maanchhe hûdaina*" (You shouldn't be too big a person), he would say.

At the same time, social aspiration and advance were clearly part of Nechung Lama's biography. He came to Kathmandu as a twelve-year-old boy in the late 1970s with a thekadaar named Tashi, who took him to a large Tibetan carpet factory in Boudhanath. There he worked for many years, eventually rising to the position of carpet master. The master in a carpet factory is responsible for dressing the carpet looms, ensuring that the weft size matches that prescribed by the design and is marked off every ten centimetres to gauge weaver productivity. Each master is responsible for supervising a number of looms and their weavers, and only accomplished and experienced weavers can become masters. They work for a fixed salary and are not paid by the piece as are the weavers. They perform a basic management function and yet are in direct proximity to the weavers from among whom they are drawn. Nechung later became his own thekadaar and returned to Uttar Banjyang to bring more weavers to the factory. He personally trained many villagers in basic carpet-weaving skills and, for a time, even started his own factory in the village. Eventually he left the factory where he worked as a master, along with many of the weavers he had trained, and with a Tibetan partner he began his own autonomous subcontracting company. After a few years he split with his partner, under what he described as acrimonious circumstances, and continued his business using the labourers he had trained in Uttar Bhanjyang.

Nechung Lama seemed to exemplify the entrepreneurial potential that is celebrated by advocates of small enterprise: informal economy, micro-credit, and social capital development, which Michael Blim (2005) calls, with some irony, "virtuous capitalism," in contradistinction to the neo-Marxist rubric of "petty capitalism." If small-scale entrepreneurs like Nechung can find a foothold in the global market, so this thinking goes, its benefits could be distributed to grassroots communities (and enrich not only global elites). Profits would be shared more equitably among locals with strong social cultural affinities that exude an ethos of communal reciprocity; wages would enrich individual households, providing sustained basic resources, shelter, education for children, and health care. However, Blim, among many others, points out that even in the case of such "virtuous capitalism," the social cost is increased inequality, which emerges along gender lines, and other aspects of hierarchies that exist within these communities. Neo-Marxist analysis correctly focuses on the subordination that many small-scale entrepreneurs experience when up against more powerful capital interests, and it suggests that they respond to this treatment by reducing labour costs to a minimum, even to the extent of exploiting under- and unpaid family or communal labour. The primordial trust of social networks does not preclude the possibility of exploitation. Even though Nechung espoused an ethos of humility and reciprocity, and no doubt believed in it, his role as an entrepreneur was structurally antagonistic to the weavers he trained in Uttar Banjyang. The problem with this view is that it offers little in the way of an analysis of how equality can be achieved. Much of the neo-Marxist literature focuses on the more blatant and reprehensible examples of the antagonism between small-scale entrepreneurs and their workers (such as debt-bondage, gender discrimination, and child labour), but ignores the extent to which small-scale entrepreneurs, like Nechung Lama, had to cultivate labour though social and symbolic reciprocity that really would be undermined by being "too big a person."

Equality was something Nechung did understand and something that he too recognized more by its absence than by its presence. During one of our regular afternoon meetings, again over sodas and cigarettes that Nechung provided, we chatted about some of the places I had been to in Helambu: how I had passed through his village on my way to Yangrima, where I had seen the stone into which Guru Rinpoche, according to local lore, had plunged his sword, similar to King Arthur's feat in European legend; how I had even been to Bodh Gaya in India and stood under the tree where the Buddha Shakyamuni had achieved enlightenment. Mulling over this immodesty, Nechung took a drag of his cigarette and said that his life was not like mine, that I was free to *gumne* around the world, meaning roughly to wander, travel, and, significantly, to circumambulate. He, on the other hand, was forced to stay in Nepal and weave carpets. Despite our frequent meetings and his earlier designation of me as aaphno maanchhe, the profound inequality that we represented was never far from his mind.

Several of the saahuji from Uttar Bhanjyang had come up with the idea of making carpet "models" for me to take back to Canada when I returned, the thought of which made me quite nervous, as my budget was already stretched and I feared the hassle of packing and shipping them home (in addition to the already considerable quantity of notes, interviews, surveys, and literature that I had collected). I told them that I was no carpet salesman, but they pressed, the idea somehow becoming diffused among them. I told them that I might take back one or two pieces to show my friends and colleagues, but not to expect any more from me. I insisted to Mingmar and Dorje that I pay for anything they made for me, reasoning that having a carpet woven would be a good opportunity to observe at close hand the weaving process. For a long time these carpet models were hypothetical, though Dorje did show me a design he said that he was working on. When Nechung casually mentioned one afternoon that he too would make a carpet for me, I was not surprised, but I suspected that he would not do so any time soon, as all of his looms were constantly occupied with program orders.

On one Friday afternoon, Shyam and I returned to our flat in Boudhanath to run through the next week's schedule before preparing for the weekend. We opened two bottles of beer that I had just bought at the corner cold store and admired the view from our balcony as the sun's intensity cooled and a pleasant evening approached. From our vantage point, Shyam spotted Nechung stepping down the steep path to our compound followed by two of his weavers, who carried a large carpet. I rushed down to meet them at the gate in order to ward off our landlord's guard dog, who seemed to distinguish visitors from potential intruders by the cut of their clothes. It regarded Nechung and his weavers wearily from its chained station and let us pass. Nechung pointed to the carpet and said that it was for me. Once on our balcony, the weaver unrolled it for everyone's inspection – a beautiful 150 × 200 cm carpet with a black central field bordered by violet and blue floral and geometric patterns. Nechung told us that this was his own design and, though the carpet was inspired by European consumer style and was not a traditional Tibetan pattern, it was indeed unlike anything that he had been weaving recently. It was appropriate that it was similar to the mass-produced carpets that the enormous industry I was studying was based on. I was both delighted and worried. Nechung refused to discuss its cost, politely refused a refreshment, and hurried out of the compound back to his factory.

The following Monday I asked Shyam about Nechung's expectations. I had insisted to Mingmar and Tsering that I pay for the small carpet they were making for me, but had neglected to do so with Nechung, sure that his early offer was hypothetical. Shyam thought that the carpet constituted a kind of *baksheesh*, a common term that signifies a gift that is intended to solicit some as yet undefined favour in return. That afternoon we made time to visit him and ask the question directly. He told us that he was thinking of the future, about perhaps finding markets for his carpets in Canada. I tried to point out that I was not the one with whom he should strike up a business relationship, that, in fact, I had learned from bitter experience that I make a rather poor salesman. He flashed a smile, told me not to worry and that it would happen only if he were lucky. He pointed to his head for emphasis.

Shyam would always draw my attention to the idiomatic use of Nepali in our interviews and discussions, the proverbial statements that he argued reflected widespread beliefs and practices that were more than individual, idiosyncratic utterances. At first he glossed Nechung's response as that he could sell carpets in Canada if he were lucky, which is how I understood it too, but later he pointed out that the idiom he used meant something somewhat different. Nechung had said he could sell carpets in Canada "if it were written in his head," which Shyam now asserted was an idiomatic statement in which luck was no random occurrence, but something that has been prefigured by fate, already decided before birth. Nechung's statement was never recorded, but I jotted it, and Shyam's interpretation, in my field notes later that evening. I did not remember the exact wording of Nechung's comment, which could have further specified my interpretation, so I was left with only the suggestion that Nechung was touching upon the boundary between oriental fatalism and Western rationalism and individual subjectivity.

In his book *Sensory Biographies* Robert Desjarlais describes a similar set of beliefs among the Yolmo in which a person's fate is thought to be "written on the skull, beneath the skin covering the forehead" (2003, 75). The idea that one's whole life and all of the events and people they encounter in it would appear as a script prefigured and set in bone at birth is intriguing, but it must have an enormous impact on how people understand actions and their consequences, because individuals are not really the authors of either. Whether things work out or not has already been decided. Desjarlais also points out that the Yolmo believe that they cannot see this script before it is put into action; it can be "read" only in retrospect and the results accepted as given.

But an adherence to fatalism no more precludes action than rational, individual subjectivity demands it. Nechung gave me a gift, and giving gifts is a risky business; accepting a gift is even more so, for gifts are rarely given without the expectation of return. One of the advantages of commodity transactions, such as paying for a carpet and thereby reducing its value to an arbitrary and negotiated value, is that they exhaust any further social expectation of return. This exchange is not so with gifts. Nechung's carpet, which is spread on the floor of my office as I write this, was intended to mark the beginning of a mutual collaboration, yet to be defined, and a calculated friendship – even if in his world view that calculation had already been made. The machinations of global carpet import and export were only dimly understood by Nechung. He had seen foreign carpet buyers arriving in their air-conditioned four-wheel-drive vehicles at the office where he obtained subcontracts, and he knew when the Tibetan exporters who awarded those subcontracts were away on business in Germany, England, Switzerland, and America. He did not know, however, how to enter that circuit; he knew how to weave carpets and how to give gifts that fasten the bonds of aaphno maanchhe. By drawing me into this collaboration, he attempted, with some success, to level the inequality that characterized our research collaboration. The risk, of course, was that what was inscribed in Nechung's head could entangle both of us in events neither of us would wish for.

Chapter Five

A Modest Chöten

Uttar Bhanjyang consists of two hamlets of about forty to fifty houses, each clustered around two small Buddhist gonpa (temples), at an altitude of about 2,000 metres, a few hours from the bazaar town of Melemchi Pul. The upper hamlet is nestled in a wood that is interspersed with dry fields on which wheat and corn are planted; the lower hamlet is situated at the top of a hillock from which Melemchi Pul is visible 1,100 metres below. Between these two hamlets, the main footpath to Helambu runs through a derelict *chöten* gate, past the recently opened public school and into a thick stand of young fir trees that were planted as part of an Australia-sponsored reforestation project in the 1970s. Inside the chöten gate are faded Buddhist frescoes that cling to crumbling plaster. A bit higher up the path, one passes a line of stone chöten that have become weathered by the rains and the years. Along one side of the ridge abandoned terraces sweep down into the valley, their owner having migrated to India. At the foot of the terraces stands an enormous, brightly painted Buddhist chöten, the characteristic dome-shaped monument found throughout the Himalayas, which is dressed with colourful prayer flags; beside it is an experimental tea plantation, an enterprise jointly undertaken by several successful local carpet merchants. Buddhist chöten not only are distinctive religious monuments, they also signal the worldly wealth and power of their benefactors. Within a single gaze, this landscape conveys the rising and passing of fortunes, the contradictions between the past and present, and the impact of history.

One afternoon I paid a visit to Nechung Lama after surveying carpet-weaving facilities in Jorpati, a peri-urban settlement on the outskirts of Kathmandu. Nechung was in his room avoiding the late afternoon heat and, as always, he offered me tea and a cigarette. Outside his window I could hear hammers striking metal, not the characteristic taps of carpet weaving, but a heavy report that echoed through the streets. Looking out, I saw a small chöten rising on a hillock beside the Bagmati River, then a shallow stream that sat motionless on the lifeless fields. I asked Nechung what was happening. He explained that this was a new *paati*, a place where families stayed for the cremation of family members, similar to those found near the Hindu temple at Pashupatinath, further downstream. He added that this paati was being built for the people of Helambu. Previously, cremations had been done at a Sherpa gonpa in Kathmandu, but doctrinal differences had led to the Sherpas' requesting that the Tamang and Yolmo lamas from Helambu conduct their cremations elsewhere. A local organizing committee, he added, was approaching people like himself for donations.

Social reciprocity is a practice that is capable of complex and nuanced symbolic communication. Gift giving implies the expectation of return and I thought that a donation to the paati project would be an opportunity to reciprocate Nechung's invaluable assistance with my research on the Tibeto-Nepalese carpet industry. Gift exchange, however, unlike straightforward commodity exchange, does not extinguish the transaction; it establishes a series of transactions, long-term alliances, and future solidarities. I suggested to Nechung that I make a donation to this project in his name, but he was cool to the proposal. Better, he said, to help build a paati for Uttar Bhanjyang, as the one outside the window was already sufficiently endowed. I warmed to Nechung's counterproposal and accepted. This was my inadvertent introduction to the internal workings of village-level politics as well as an object lesson in how traditional forms of reciprocity are, and perhaps always have been, motivated in part by individual interest – the seeking of wealth, influence, and prestige. My contribution to the paati project was but the next in a long (and ongoing) series of gifts and counter-gifts, expectations and counter-expectations, in which altruism and calculation are not easily distinguished.

Nechung was delighted with my offer and said that he would organize a meeting of the village panchayat to discuss the project. The panchayat to which he referred meant not the men who comprised the political administration of the village through the Village Development Committee (VDC), representatives of political parties elected by popular franchise, but the traditional body of lamas who still were in control of

Figure 5.1. Young men in Uttar Bhanjyang putting the final touches on a chöten, October 1998.

guthi lands – grants of land made to religious leaders by previous Nepalese governments – on which Nechung planned to build. His idea was to construct a small paati, a three-walled concrete shelter with space for sleeping and cooking, to house visiting families or lamas who must preside over the funerary puja. In front of the paati we would also build a modest chöten – Nechung held his hand to his shoulder to indicate its height – that would mark the space as hallowed ground. We agreed to meet again in Uttar Bhanjyang for the meeting of the panchayat during the Dasain festival in a few weeks time to formalize our plans. Though Dasain is a Hindu festival, the Buddhist lamas of Uttar Bhanjyang were obligated to perform puja during that period by the government of Chandra Shumsher Rana, a condition for the grant of their guthi lands. In any case, Nechung's carpet factory would be closed for two weeks to allow his workers to return to their villages for the festival, and, as our fieldwork was drawing to a close, we could make a trek to Yangrima and beyond into the Langtang range of the Himalayas.

As Dasain approached, we trekked up Helambu from the Melemchi Valley in a shroud of lingering monsoon clouds that turned the only trail to Uttar Bhanjyang into a leech-infested stream of mud. Once in the village, Nechung and his family were nowhere to be found, so we huddled by the fire in the small lodge where we were to rendezvous, trying to ward off the unseasonable dampness. By late afternoon, the clouds had parted slightly, giving a view of the bronze spire of the gonpa on a hill above us, while the unmistakable drone of puja chanting drifted down through the mist. We climbed up to investigate. Once we were there, an older man dressed in red robes motioned for us to enter. The inside of the gonpa was bathed in butter-lamp light and filled with sweet incense smoke. At the front of the group was what appeared to be a child's doll, placed squarely under an effigy of Guru Rinpoche, the saint who brought Tantric Buddhism to Tibet 1,200 years ago and a *bodhisattva* who deferred his own enlightenment out of compassion for the suffering of others. The bronze statue of the guru, sometimes known by his Sanskrit name, Padmasambhava, was wrapped with coloured cloth and a ceremonial khata darkened by ash and smoke. I knew that these silk scarves were supposed to represent the many different robes that he wore, one from each of his teachers, which symbolized the transmission of a teaching, of a tradition. As I studied the guru, a number of men chanted from long, loose-leaf books of Tibetan script, while several villagers sat passively on the floor, as if lost in thought. A young man approached us and began to narrate the proceedings in English, in which he was perhaps no more competent than I was in Nepali. He explained that this was a puja being given for a baby who had died of a fever en route to Uttar Bhanjyang just the day before. Uttar Bhanjyang had no health post, he explained, and it was too late to get the baby back to Kathmandu. I looked again at a young woman sitting in the centre of the group with her eyes of glass and head held sadly, stoically. I recognized her – she was a weaver in Nechung's carpet factory whom I had earlier studied while she worked at her loom. We had blundered into a funeral, intruded into a private rite of grieving. We sat for a few minutes, then quietly stole out the door.

Another woman hurried out, motioning us to follow. We were led to a mud-brick house and onto a tattered bamboo mat beside an open hearth that belched black smoke. Our hostess was Nechung's sister. We were given glasses of smooth but potent raksi, the local country liquor distilled from millet or rice beer, and a plate of *sukuti*, meat that was dried and then roasted, a particular delicacy during Dasain. After a few minutes, Nechung arrived with his family, and many of the mourners from the gonpa followed, including the grieving mother. The atmosphere from then on was far from sombre. We drank and talked for about an hour.

The *sukuti* tasted familiar. I asked Nechung what kind of meat it was, and he told me that a tiger had come out of the jungle and killed a cow. We were eating the leftovers. He smiled, a few others chuckled, then the chuckles built into general laughter. Cow killing, we all knew, was still illegal in officially Hindu Nepal. The tiger story, though blatantly untrue (there were no tigers in the area, as the heavily terraced hillsides left little in the way of jungle for them to lurk in), qualified the meat as carrion, which legally could be consumed. It tasted delicious.

After some time the panchayat meeting began on the outside porch with several of the lamas who had presided over the funeral puja. Nechung ran off into the mist to fetch a fifth member of the committee so that our meeting would reach quorum. The rest of the committee stared at me, lighting up occasionally as if to start a conversation, then falling silent as I strained to penetrate their thick accents. I fumbled for a torch with which to illuminate the meeting, as the two goats who shared the porch with us nosed through my backpack. Nechung returned, quorum was met, tea was served, and the discussions began. The lamas engaged in vigorous debate, raising their voices to each other, gesticulating with their hands, pounding the ground with their fists. I sat helplessly observing, not being able to follow the controversy. Nechung summed up some of the discussion into a number of points that he asked me to write, in English, in my journal. There was considerable debate over the quantity of materials, the amount of time, and number of people required. All that I was to write in my journal was a total figure of 35,000 rupees (about $1,000 CAD), and an undertaking that I would pay this amount in three instalments, the first now and the next two over the course of the next year.

35,000 rupees was more than twice the sum I had originally offered to Nechung and well beyond what my meagre research budget contained. How this amount came to be inflated I did not understand, as through much of the meeting the men had been speaking rapidly in a local Tibetan dialect that I did not speak. It was only after Nechung explained to me in slow and carefully enunciated Nepali, as though I were hard of hearing, that I grasped what they were asking of me. I could have protested but did not, as the sum, when divided into instalments, did not seem too onerous. I requested that the agreement that I was writing be signed, as I was required to submit receipts when I returned to the university. I signed, as did Nechung and two others. The last three dipped their thumbs in ashes that were retrieved from the hearth upstairs and fixed their mark to the bottom of the document. With our business done, more raksi appeared, but we excused ourselves and went back to rest in order to continue the trek to Yangrima the following day.

We set off the next morning, the clouds having lifted and the bright autumn sun finally shining down. Climbing into the trees just the other side of the village, we stopped at the cluster of about ten or fifteen weathered chöten. An older man followed us at a distance, balancing himself on his walking stick. He smiled at us as he passed, then stopped and pointed up the hill. "Yangrima?" he asked. "Yes," I replied. I then managed to ask him about the chöten. He told me that there had been 108 here at one time, some quite large, but most small: "the rich people get the big ones, while the poor have to content themselves with the small." On the other side of the path, there had been a massive landslip, and a number of ancient chöten, both rich and poor, must have fallen into the Indrawati Valley, an object lesson in the impermanence of human endeavour. Once monuments to past prestige, the chöten decayed and tumbled into the valley, along with memories of their builders. We walked on together for a few minutes before he turned down a side path and waved.

In the interval between making the agreement to begin the paati project and its completion two years later, Nechung's business was dealt a blow by the global carpet market that made it difficult for many small-scale entrepreneurs to compete. Nechung closed his factory and returned with his family to Uttar Bhanjyang until he was confident that he could find orders again. Indeed, most small-scale entrepreneurs were similarly flexible, often returning to their villages during off periods or dabbling in other economic activities, usually in the informal sector, in order to survive between times. The paati project gave Nechung some focus, and he spent some time in Uttar Bhanjyang organizing its construction. In addition to this endeavour, Nechung commissioned a metal sign that identified the spot where, in Uttar Bhanjyang legend, NgaCha Shakya Zangpo, the Tantric Buddhist founder of the Yolmo lineages that populated the Helambu region, used his magical powers to break through the earth with his staff to create the spring that supplies the village with fresh, clean water. The sign identifies the village as the "Heart of

Helambu," in both English and Nepali, and directs the reader to visit the village of Uttar Bhanjyang and the paati. My name is also featured on the plaque as the principal contributor to the chöten and paati in the village. Nechung's designation of this spot as the "Heart of Helambu" struck me as curious, as, according to Graham Clarke's (1980) history of the region, as well as ethnographies by Robert Desjarlais (1992), Naomi Bishop (1998), and others, the heart of Helambu ought to lie further to the north in Tarke Ghyang, which is not only a geographical centre for the area, but a cultural one as well. Bishop puts the southern boundary of what she considers Helambu about twenty minutes uphill. At best, Uttar Bhanjyang lies at the southernmost extremity of this cultural region, yet Nechung's sign, written in both Nepali and English, designates this spot as its centre.

Nechung postponed the formal ceremony that would officially inaugurate the paati until I was able to return to Nepal in 1998, to conduct research on carpet labourers, wages, and remittances. Once again our journey to Helambu was greeted with unseasonable chill and rain. We knew that our arrival in Uttar Bhanjyang was imminent after we came to the place where in legend the village began – a red metal sign announcing that the stream we were crossing was the "Heart of Helambu." From this source, the stream flowed down the hill to join the Indrawati River and away from Uttar Bhanjyang. We climbed up past fields of millet to the saddle that separated the two hamlets that comprised the village. It was getting dark as we reached the guest house where we were to be fed and put up for the night. Without a word, Nechung disappeared as we ate our dinner under the gaze of our host, a reticent and thoughtful man named Sonam.

I initially mistook Sonam to be vaguely cool to our presence, but came to understand that he was a man of few words but of many actions. Nechung soon returned with a jar of warm milk, just obtained from a cow, which was creamy and delicious. Sonam then offered a "little little" in a conspiratorial manner, squeezing his thumb and forefinger together in a familiar gesture. These were the only English words that I ever heard him utter. "Little little" was a neologism, invented perhaps for our benefit, which referred to sharing several glasses of potent raksi. After a few small glasses of this millet moonshine we all accompanied Sonam up the hill, in the dark, to admire a brand new guest house that he was soon to complete. Sonam was a carpenter and, like many men living in the area, a migrant worker who had returned to Uttar Bhanjyang from India with, unlike most others perhaps, sufficient capital to mount this enterprise. He was also the currently elected head of the Village Development Committee – effectively the mayor of Uttar Bhanjyang, elected under the banner of the Communist Party of Nepal (Marxist-Leninist).

Figure 5.2. Nechung's sign guiding trekkers to the "Heart of Helambu," October 1998.

The next morning we had our tea and looked outside as black monsoon clouds lumbered over and beside the guest lodge, so close that we could almost reach out and touch them. It looked as though the ceremony would have to be held in a downpour. A contingent of people, led by one of the men whom I recognized had presided over the panchayat meeting two years earlier, came through the fog and summoned us up the hill. Sonam told us to wait, however, as the ground was roiling with cold rain. After an hour it became apparent that the monsoon would not subside for our benefit, so we climbed up the hill to the paati site, where a large crowd of people was waiting under the steel roof of the main concrete building. People rushed out to escort us up the stone steps to where a red ribbon was stretched across the entrance gate. Ceremonial khata were placed around my neck, so many that they were piled over the top of my head. Someone pressed a pair of metal scissors into my hand, the same kind used by weavers to shape and tenter their carpets in Kathmandu. I cut the ribbon, not unlike any municipal official in any jurisdiction anywhere opening a shopping mall, a school, or a public park. This ceremony clearly had no religious significance, though it was important for several of the key participants for whom it had political value.

We climbed the steps to the paati ground. An enormous chöten towered overhead, freshly painted and garlanded with hundreds of multi-coloured prayer flags. The modest chöten that Nechung had described two years earlier had grown in size, in ambition, and in cost. This chöten towered five metres high atop a tree-ringed hillock, and thirteen elegant rings that represented the thirteen stages of enlightenment lifted the double symbol of the sun and moon into the overcast sky. Cradled within the concave moon was a brightly painted tongue of flame, the *bindu*, which, according to tradition, was the last feature to be completed on the chöten. Though I was aware of the religious symbolism of the monument, its social and political importance seemed to be a priority in the context of this day. As I was led around it, I clutched a notebook in which I had written the romanized version of a speech that I was to give to the substantial number of people huddled inside the paati. This would be my first attempt at public speaking in Nepali and would be given to a community of people for whom Nepali was a second language. I knew that Nechung had also prepared a speech, but he had given few guidelines for what was expected of mine.

We were directed to sit to one side of three lamas who were already ensconced behind a low bench on which lay bowls of coloured powder, loose-leaf Tibetan texts, ceremonial bells, and *dorje* (bronze symbols of a thunderbolt), all to be used in puja. These men were not introduced to us. Instead, we were directed to shake hands with a short man named Tsering Lama, impeccably dressed and with every shining hair on his head in place. In his pressed and spotless attire Tsering looked incongruous among the rest of us, as we were soaked by rain and drenched in mud, but it was with him that we consulted about the order of events, this ceremony appearing to be improvised on the spot. One of the lamas struggled to maintain order among the children who pushed to the front of the group, but with little effect.

After a few photographs, for which everyone posed in the typically severe fashion I had noticed in family snapshots that were often shown to me, the well-heeled Tsering began to speak over a cacophony of voices that reluctantly subsided. After a perfunctory greeting to all, he reported on the accounts for the project, pointing out that a total of 80,000 rupees had been spent, including 32,000 rupees donated by myself, another 34,000 from Nechung, and 14,000 raised from people in the village. By the time he finished the crowd was quiet and Sonam provided a few words of welcome. I found the order of events to be odd – who was this Tsering, and why was a precise accounting of the project so important as to receive top billing? Nechung then followed, giving an inspired speech about the importance of community development and the responsibility that people like him had towards providing service. His voice was full, projected from his diaphragm, and his eyes were filled with tears.

Before I could speak, I was given two butter lamps and told to circumambulate the chöten. As directed, I placed one lamp on its northern side, and on my way around, on the south side, I found a framed picture of the Buddha, similar to those readily found in local bookshops and markets in Kathmandu, and a portrait of King Birendra and Queen Aishwara. I placed a butter lamp among them. Just below, I saw for the first time a plaque of engraved marble that detailed the same summary of accounts given by Tsering, which was titled, in both Nepali and English, "Service Is Religion." My wife and I were listed as "Canadian friends" and Nechung as a "local social helper." It struck me as I saw this, that this was the first time, in all of my travels in Nepal that I had ever seen such an accounting fixed to a chöten or stupa. Whereas in the past such acknowledgment was implied or was a fact of local knowledge, in the present it seemed, charity was subject to standards of accountability, so that there could be no mistaking to whom merit was due.

I returned to give my speech, in which I stressed that my donation was a gift given in recognition of Nechung's assistance to my research, and a hope that the cooperation shown by all would mean more development in the future. I used the Nepalese word *bikas* (development) here, as Nechung had also done in his own speech, aware that people were not understanding it with the irony that I had been taught (see Pigg 1992). "Bikas" is a term by which the Nepalese state means modernizing key areas of Nepalese society and economy: improving agricultural production and education and building the infrastructure for a modern state. Nanda Shrestha (2008) describes bikas as "winds of change" that are transforming peasant life for the worse throughout the Nepal Himalayas. The state's interest and the interest of global capital in progressive development are often narrated as being in the best interests of the poor, but the same people thought to benefit from it too often suffer the consequences of change.

There was not much wind that day in Uttar Bhanjyang; there was only a dense cold rain that filled the concrete shelter with chill. Using bikas in my speech did not reflect a critical position on the concept because, pragmatically, it was not appropriate to do so. My use of the word was consistent with how it was used locally. Bikas, in popular usage, means new schools, roads, electricity, hospitals or health posts, jobs, consumer goods, and a teleology that only gets better. For Nechung and the people gathered that day the paati project was a concrete example of that progress. Once I had concluded my speech and everyone had applauded enthusiastically, one of the elder lamas turned to Tsering and asked, "What did he say?" Tsering then rose to translate my speech for the assembled audience. The crowd ignored his reiteration and Tsering relented as they flooded outside. I noticed that the rear corner of the paati had already developed a long crack and that bits of wet concrete lay in a pile on the floor. The proceedings drew to a close and a general sense of celebration ensued, with people perhaps relieved not to have to hear more speeches. Photographs were posed for and taken as a final puja was given under the chöten.

As the crowd thinned, Tsering Lama approached and offered us, once again in English, a "little little" and motioned towards the village gonpa. Nechung and Sonam also were invited, but Sonam, who had assumed the role of host, was reluctant for us to go, explaining that his wife was preparing a meal for us. He was finally convinced, in the local Yolmo dialect, and, despite his reservations, we headed to the gonpa for a drink. We entered and sat down behind two low wooden tables under the eyes of Guru Rinpoche. Sonam and I sat on one side, Nechung and a group of younger men on the other. The three lamas who led the puja sat directly under the gonpa altar. One of them leapt up to chase away a group of children who had taken the opportunity of this unconventional use of the temple to play a game of tag, or its local variant, among wooden columns lavishly painted with patterns and symbols. He brandished a switch at them, but they ignored it, and he sat down, resigned to their game. The children left of their own accord as several Chinese tea flasks of sweet tea appeared, followed by kettles of warm raksi that Tsering announced was of the highest quality, not contaminated by aftertastes of kerosene as was often the case in Kathmandu.

Tsering, it seemed, wanted an opportunity to volunteer as an expert informant, and again he recounted the story of Shakya Lama's magical power, the same tale that I had read on Nechung's sign just below the village, adding the detail that the massive pipal tree growing near the site sprang from the staff that Shakya Lama had thrust into the ground. He went on elaborating on the history of the gonpa, which sits on guthi land, how it was felled by the earthquake of 1934, destroyed by fire some years later, and finally rebuilt. The three lamas who presided over the gonpa sat passively, listening and sipping their drinks.

Tsering shifted his monologue from guthi history to guthi administration. The three lamas chatted among themselves softly as if to signal their disinterest in Tsering's tale. He then spoke directly to them, urging them to consider registering the guthi with the government. I turned to Sonam for an explanation and he whispered that doing so would mean that a committee or board would have to be constituted to oversee its budget. Everyone looked to the three lamas, who were staring at the floor. Tsering then exclaimed that 30,000 rupees, a grant that had been obtained to refurbish the gonpa, had recently been "eaten by them." He pointed to the lamas in accusation, his finger quivering in the air. The lamas displayed no emotion, but only sipped their raksi and drew on their cigarettes.

A long silence ensued. Tsering then said that the older lamas were refusing to register their guthi, as it would mean that they would lose their jobs. He laughed, as if in triumph, but no one joined in. I looked longingly at the gonpa door. Tsering motioned to a young man nearby to refill my glass and formally asked me to make a further donation to the guthi. Did he want the 30,000 rupees from me? I gave a non-committal response, truly confused about what was being requested and what it meant to the others sitting in the room, but mostly about how to get out of there. The raksi began to take effect. I raised the glass and only wetted my lips with it. I needed to stay in control.

There was a commotion outside and Nechung's wife appeared at the door. Nechung and Sonam lifted me to my feet, explained that our dinner was ready, and hustled me outside. There was, in fact, no meal being prepared for us. Sonam and Nechung led us instead onto the porch of a house to escape the driving rain. Both were perplexed by the impromptu meeting in the gonpa and had had no forewarning of Tsering's request, which we were advised to ignore. Nechung remarked that Tsering was a *"chiplo maanchhe"* (slippery person) and performed an impression of his guileful mannerisms, slicking back his curly hair and whistling *"namaste, sahib"* through his teeth as Tsering had done. Everyone was amused by this, even the normally reserved Sonam chuckled, showing a gold incisor. Another man appeared at the door of the house, motioning for us to enter. Another metal kettle of raksi appeared. People continued to speak about Tsering, about how he was the former head of the VDC and recently had been defeated in his re-election bid by none other than Sonam. Sonam was a member of the Communist Party of Nepal (UML), while the defeated Tsering belonged to the Rastriya Prajantantra Party of former panchayat loyalists who sought a return to a government dominated by the nobility and, by extension, Nepal's traditional elites.

Sonam claimed that Tsering's appeal for a donation to the local guthi was politically motivated, an analysis that everyone eagerly shared. Since Sonam was allied to Nechung and in partial receipt of the cultural capital that flowed from my donation, Tsering was attempting to make his own mark. Moreover, Tsering's accusation of fiscal impropriety, directed at the lamas who oversaw the gonpa and its extensive guthi lands, demonstrates how the seemingly modern value of accountability can become a tool for local political leverage. The notion that government funds are public and must be put to use in an open and accountable way is particularly and peculiarly rational and bureaucratic – it also clashes fundamentally with traditional channels of distribution common in Nepal. Tsering's statement that the lamas "ate" the funds may not be far off the mark, as guthi lands are often cultivated by hereditary lamas who have influence with the gonpa, but it is also merely a claim that he himself had received no direct benefit from these funds. Alex Kondos (1987) points out that traditional favouritism, the "source and force" that flows from social alliances, is considered "corruption" in urban Kathmandu only by those who are outside those alliances; that is, they consider their own claims to "source and force" to be legitimate (see also Justice 1986). This is more the case in Uttar Bhanjyang, and thus the announcement of accounts for the paati project, inscribed in marble, are a unique buffer against the sort of criticism that Tsering levelled at the lamas.

The rain ended, finally, and the sun reappeared. Steam rose from the ground and off the roofs of the houses. Sonam led us outside where we took some more photographs. He proudly drew our attention to a communal water tap, surrounded by a bright garden. It was, he told us, one of the new taps that the village had built with state funds in 1994, the year that the short-lived CPN (UML) government had instituted a program called *aaphno gaû, aapno banaaû* – roughly, "let's build our own village" – which dispersed large grants from the public purse to each VDC in the country to use as it saw fit. Sonam used the funds to organize the building of a central spring-sourced tank located behind the gonpa, which fed a number of taps in the village, alleviating the need for women to walk some distance to carry water to their homes. The water tap was not Shakya Lama's powerful staff, perhaps, but was its modern counterpart. Both the RPP and the Nepal Congress Party had accused the then governing UML of using state funds illegitimately to shore up Communist support in the villages, showing once again that legitimacy is an ambiguous and politicized concept in the Nepal Himalayas.

As we returned to our lodge through the millet fields around the paati, one of our companions, a weaver in Nechung's Jorpati factory, turned to a friend and said, "now we have our own foreigner," implying that I was somehow a key to village development. Apparently, Tsering Lama had unsuccessfully tried to recruit me as "his" foreigner, but the weaver's statement confirmed that I belonged to Nechung, Sonam, and their people. I was to be their agent of bikas, a source of future support, investment, and assistance. This was a responsibility that I was not sure how to live up to.

Having spent so much time on the ceremony and its consequences, I felt a strong urge to return to my fieldwork proper. I had with me a list of questions that I had composed in Canada a few months earlier and translated into romanized Nepali after our arrival in Kathmandu. These questions pertained to migration to Kathmandu, labour bondage, and carpet labour contracting, and they reflected issues that arose from the background reading I had been doing. The list felt inadequate in the light of what I had discovered more recently: the political schisms that democracy had opened in Uttar Bhanjyang and, of course, the local controversies that had been exposed by the paati project. However, these discoveries did not appear to pertain to my fieldwork. I began by interviewing many of the participants of the inauguration ceremony, as many of them had extensive connections with Kathmandu and the carpet industry in Boudhanath. In order to break the ice with several of the older villagers, I led off the discussion with questions about Shakya Lama and the origins of the village. Each person who related the story to me did so with minor variations: in some, Shakya Lama thrust his staff into the ground to release the spring water; in others, the staff was misplaced, and the pipal tree that marks the village spring marks the spot where it was lost. One of the panchayat members told me about Shakya Lama's magical powers to protect crops from hailstorms and that there was a place at the bottom of the village where his footprint was impressed in rock. Sensing that this material, though interesting, was peripheral to my research interests, I always gently refocused the discussion on the issues under investigation, even though I would have much preferred to have heard about Shakya Lama.

Rinzen Lama, a young man who previously had woven carpets in Nechung's factory and whom I was now employing as a local assistant, arranged for us to interview a number of villagers who had left carpet weaving in Kathmandu and returned to Uttar Banjyang, which was the ultimate objective of our visit there. This focus group, of about a dozen people, was extraordinarily fruitful, lasting most of the afternoon. The group contained people with strong opinions and an ability to express them far more eloquently than many of the weavers we had been working with in Kathmandu. My own confidence in my ability to conduct interviews in Nepali had also grown to the extent that now I was able to engage far more with these weavers than in the past, though we all struggled with our heavily accented variations of the language. I knew that this interview was one of the most important that I had collected so far and I hungered for more. We had only one day remaining before we needed to return to Kathmandu and it promised to be a productive one. After the interview ended, people lingered, chatting and drinking tea. I turned to Rinzen and asked whether he could arrange for another session tomorrow with some other weavers. His reply was without hesitation, "There is no one else, sir." "No one?" I was deflated. The harvest needed to be brought in and people could not afford the time away. Besides, Rinzen said, there were only one or two weavers left and they lived too far from Uttar Bhanjyang. There were few prospects for the next day, but Rinzen was still on contract as a research assistant and I did not want to deny him his wages. We returned to his house for tea, where it occurred to me how to fill the time, "Can you take me to see Shakya Lama's footprint?" I asked. He agreed with some excitement, which I partly shared, though this was tempered by a concern that my time was running short, and that I needed to make sure I allowed enough time to complete the work that my research on carpet weavers and their wages required. I was unsure about how this journey to explore an aspect of Uttar Bhanjyang's history would contribute to my overall reason for being there, but was enthusiastic to try.

The next morning we met and, after a meal served by Rinzen's mother, we set off in the company of two of his friends who were also curious to see Shakya Lama's footprint. We descended the hillside on dusty trails rutted by monsoon rainwater to a stand of trees that Rinzen called the "jungle," but that was actually a tract grown as part of an Australian reforestation project. The young pine trees were planted in neat rows, and most of the trees along the footpath had been stripped nearly to the top for fodder and firewood. When we emerged from the other side of this "jungle," the terrain began to level off as it fell, gently, to the Melemchi River a few hundred metres away. We were no longer in Buddhist Helambu, having crossed into other Village Development Committee land, which was inhabited predominantly by Hindu Brahmins and Chetris.

Rinzen led us to a rock cairn on the side of the hill and thrust his head into the opening at the front. He began to fling rocks and debris – bits of wood, discarded cans, and torn plastic bags – from inside, as a woman carrying a basket along the footpath stopped to watch in amazement. I lifted my camera to take a photograph of the cairn. Fearing that she would be included in the shot, the woman barked at me that she did not want her picture taken. I told her that only the cairn was in my frame. Rinzen then emerged from his work and spun around to her, brandishing a wrapper of dried noodles in his hand. "This is our *mani*," he said, "and you people put your garbage in it!" The woman snorted something and walked off.

We all pitched in and helped to remove the debris from inside the cairn, eventually revealing a thin slab of sandstone. Rinzen swept the remaining layer of dust from it. I did not know what to expect.

Perhaps it would be something clearly manufactured, such as the footprints of the Buddha that I had seen in India and Thailand, or perhaps there was some natural feature that a stretch of the imagination could conjure into a footprint. But there, clearly, unmistakably, was the impression of a human foot. A tiny left footprint, as though made by a child.

I asked Rinzen why there was only one. The other footprint, the right foot, he told me, was located just above Tarkhe Ghyang to the north. From a local perspective, then, the place known as Helambu was straddled in Shakya Lama's stride. Here, however, one of his feet was in estranged territory, in another village now populated by Brahmin and Chetris farmers. The cairn showed signs of neglect, and the fact that we discovered so much rubbish inside was a sign that no one had paid much recent attention to it. One of Rinzen's friends then called our attention to one of the fragments of rock that had been pulled out of the cairn. It was clearly a carved mani (prayer stone), though the small Tibetan characters on it were badly eroded by the elements. I watched as the other three tried to read it, stumbling and debating over the meaning of the words. Rinzen could tell me only that it seemed to be about Shakya Lama's story, but he admitted that their knowledge of the language was not sufficient to read the mani with any more accuracy.

Before we left the cairn, Rinzen replaced the mani inside, propped up behind Shakyai Lama's footprint. As we returned, and ever since, I have wondered and worried about the significance of this event. Was this experience merely for collection, a way to fulfil a contract obligation that bears little significance for my own professional project? In retrospect, the significance of our day rests not so much on the footprint itself, but how we found it, a neglected and nearly forgotten marker of local collective identity.

Many people from Uttar Bhanjyang now have an outward orientation, towards Kathmandu, the carpet industry, and new households taking root in Boudhanath and Jorpati; also towards India, where many have gone for employment or education, as well as, most recently, towards the shifting frontiers of transnational labour in the Persian Gulf states of Southeast Asia. In many ways Uttar Bhanjyang is a place rooted in the past, a place that is both inadequate to the growing aspirations of its young inhabitants and a place of refuge for those, like Nechung Lama, who retreat there from time to time when those aspirations are thwarted. His insistence on building his paati there, the project that he drew me into, was not only a calculated effort to increase his own prestige and cultural capital, nor was it only an effort to accrue religious merit, as he easily could have accomplished those aims in Kathmandu. It was also, I now recognize, an effort to recover a place that is in his heart. A place that he, and many others in Uttar Bhanjyang, feared would be lost as their lives extend beyond a landscape on which their cultural history has been inscribed.

This insight was gained only by briefly abandoning purposive fieldwork activity and improvising on opportunities made available by immediate circumstance. I would have learned little of this state of affairs had it not been for asking a benign question about the sound of hammering heard through Nechung's window in Kathmandu. Nechung, along with most other carpet weavers and entrepreneurs, had always articulated a strong sense of connection to his village, even though he lived mostly in the city. While I had studied the considerable flow of remittances from urban weavers to their families in Nepal's hill and *tarai* (lowland) villages, and understood the importance of these villages as sources of cheap labour for Kathmandu's industries, the sequence of events precipitated by this question led me to understand the affective depth, and ambiguous force, of the place of the village in the imagination and practice of urban migrants. For them, the village is an intermittently inhabited space in which there is danger that much will be forgotten in exchange for what is hoped to be gained in the city. This at least was the case for Nechung, but I suspect it is also true for many migrants living in peri-urban Kathmandu and perhaps as well for those in many of the other rapidly urbanizing regions in the globalizing world.

Chapter Six

Diverging Paths

After my return to Canada things began to unravel for Nechung and most of the small-scale carpet makers from Helambu. The carpet industry that drew him from his home in Uttar Bhanjyang as a child and provided him with an opportunity to fashion a better life for his family as an autonomous subcontractor stopped its rapid growth and began to decline after 1996. By the year 2000 many small subcontractors had folded, including those from Uttar Bhanjyang. Nechung's friend Dorje Lama finally closed his unsuccessful factory and went into retreat in a cave. Another neighbour struggled with a debt of 7 *lakh* (700,000) rupees after the eldest son, who ran a factory in Jorpati, died suddenly, leaving not only the debt, but a child who continued to be boarded in Kathmandu to attend school. Heavy debt loads were not uncommon. The fact that most of those debts were not held by formal financial institutions made matters worse, for either they grew out of control because of usurious interest rates charged by informal money lenders or they strained relationships where capital was raised from family and friends. Subcontractors like Nechung who maintained close ties with large, established exporters were on firmer ground, but even that was giving way. As numbers of carpet orders decreased, exporters became less reliant on putting work out to subcontractors.

At first Nechung seemed to sustain his business, but the situation soon began to slide. His letters to me became more fraught and his email messages more frequent, often chiding me for the irregularity of my letters to him, even though the interval between our correspondences was not unusually lengthy. He sold his motorcycle, withdrew his children from the school that they were enrolled in, and was forced to lay off most of his workers. To make matters worse, he told me that the paati had been seriously damaged by the monsoon and was in danger of collapsing. Though all of this news was increasingly desperate, he never explicitly asked for money. I suspected that an expectation of aid went unspoken, because to put it directly into words would violate the subtle rules of reciprocity.

Our fortunes diverged in the years after the 1998 fieldwork. I found a full-time faculty job in 1999 and bought a house, a car, and a dog. I settled into the trying routine of full-time professorial work: designing courses, supervising students, writing articles, attending conferences, sitting on committees, and trying to keep abreast of the rapid changes in Nepal's fragile political situation from a distracted and sheltered distance. We were expecting our first child. After years of struggling as a graduate student and as an unemployed scholar, I was beginning to be comfortable.

One day in early 2000 I found a letter from Nechung in my mailbox, registered, as they generally were, and emblazoned with a number of stamps announcing Nepal as the birthplace of the Buddha. I tore one end away and pulled out the letter. A small postcard that bore a picture of Guru Rinpoche fell to the floor. Picking it up, I noticed an annotation scrawled on the back, "In memory of my son, Pruba Kalsang Lama, 1989–2000." I immediately examined Nechung's ghostwritten letter for details. Pruba, Nechung's ten-year-old son had died, he wrote, "because of stomach problems." This news was shocking. I looked at a framed photograph that I kept on my desk of Nechung, Shyam, Narendra, and their families attending a picnic at Balaju just before we left Nepal two years earlier. Pruba is in the front row of the posed picture, just behind Shyam's daughter, smiling mischievously as he held a two-finger sign behind her head.

The photograph was a necessary mnemonic, as I had had precious little contact with Nechung's two children while in Nepal. Occasionally, they were paraded before us to recount some school event or torn from their play by their mother to pay an obeisant "Namaste, uncle" before escaping back to their games, but there had been little unmediated interaction with the children or women. I now regretted this. The thought of losing a child horrified me. I hadn't yet found the time to write Nechung to let him know about the forthcoming birth of our own child, and that normally joyful task now filled me with dread.

Pruba had been ill for a number of years and was often home from school when I first began working with Nechung. I had never asked about what the problem was with the boy. Nechung's domestic life was something that had rarely entered into our conversations, as these were generally between men, over cigarettes and salt tea. Nechung's wife, Maya, and daughter, Phulmaya, participated in these conversations only in a supporting role, pouring tea when required, preparing momo, hovering inconspicuously on the margins of the male sphere. I was a part of that sphere into which women and children, or their concerns, were rarely admitted. Production and social reproduction overlapped to a great extent, particularly in small-scale industries, but I saw household and family matters as subordinate, as it was in much of my dialogue with Nechung and other Nepalis. Pruba's death laid bare the patriarchal myopia in which I had unwittingly participated. It also presented problems concerning how I was to respond, both directly to Nechung and his family and in my own work. The two are inextricably linked.

I sent Nechung some money to repair the paati and told him that this donation was in Pruba's memory. It seemed the least that I could do under the circumstances. I knew that this donation, however, would

Figure 6.1. The completed chöten in Uttar Bhanjyang, October 1998.

not exhaust my obligation to Nechung and his family, that I could not retreat into transnational indifference. We both were subjects of a co-created relationship that was embedded in forces that cast us in roles that undermined that relationship. Pruba's death underscored the disparity of our lives, for though I was not certain about the cause of his death, I suspected that the poor health care available even to those who could afford it played a part in his death. The local health clinic in Jorpati was ill equipped to handle a condition that would likely have required extensive diagnosis and treatment, and local hospitals provided care at an expense that Nechung could not afford as his livelihood dwindled along with European carpet demand.

The only other member of the family with whom I had developed any sort of relation was Phulmaya. Like her brothers, Phulmaya tended to remain in the background earlier in my fieldwork and was even less conspicuous because she had, and has, an extensive network of friends that kept her away from the house. Later we came to know more of her as she grew, and she became a valuable assistant to my wife. Phulmaya was an extremely extroverted young woman, much in contrast to her more reserved parents, and this sociability made it possible to see their household from her perspective. She was also ambitious and eager to break free of the limitations and constraints that bedevilled her parents. Shortly after Pruba's death, Phulmaya had obtained a contract to work as a domestic servant in Kuwait and left Kathmandu for two years. She found the job through a shadowy labour broker and had to travel first to India in order to bypass authorities in Nepal, as at that time it was illegal for women to migrate abroad, alone, for work. To Phulmaya, this legal restriction was but an obstacle to her goals, which were shared by her parents, who gave her the money to pay the hefty fees charged by the broker. Nechung no doubt hoped that she would be able to send money home. Living in Kathmandu, he had been asked many times to deliver letters from Kuwait to other households in Uttar Bhanjyang when he returned there, and he was aware of the value of the remittances that these households received from their daughters in Kuwait. The gambit of sending Phulmaya failed when she returned after only one year of the two-year commitment. After that, Nechung's precarious financial condition deteriorated further.

I made plans to do a very short field visit to Kathmandu in June 2001 in order to speak with Phulmaya and her friends about their experiences in Kuwait, in hopes of engaging in an emerging debate in social anthropology around female transnational migration, particularly for domestic labour, which figured the female migrant as a globalized, subaltern subject and the remittance economy a commoditization of family relationships (see, e.g., Constable 1997; Parreñas 2001). Did Phulmaya and the many young women from Uttar Bhanjyang who also evaded public authority to work in the Persian Gulf fit this same pattern?

A few days before my departure, Crown Prince Dipendra, King Birendra's son and heir to the Shah dynasty, went on a drug-fuelled rampage and killed his father, mother, brothers, sisters, and himself, throwing into turmoil the official elites that had dominated Nepal for over 200 years. The dying crown prince, the murderer, was officially named king after his father passed away, exposing the confusion and desperation of Nepal's elites, as the world they had dominated for so long succumbed as well to the hail of automatic-weapon fire. Virtual Nepal – that is, the news websites, chat rooms, and blogs – began to circulate various conspiracy theories about the killings, pointing to the late king's brother, or his playboy son, or the Maoist insurgents, or the Indian government as the culprit(s). Kathmandu was convulsed by rioting in the days that followed as people sought to grasp the shocking event, and I was forced to delay my departure until the situation had settled down. By the time I reached Kathmandu a month later, the city had returned to some semblance of normality, though it was sandbagged and surrounded by razor wire. Military vehicles ferrying soldiers and police were everywhere, and camouflaged patrols strutted along the Ring Road, nervously watching the crowds.

Nechung met me at the airport in the company of several people whom I had not met. Once we were in the taxi, he informed me that Phulmaya had left to take a job in Dubai a few weeks before. Word could not be sent to me before I left. I was distressed at this bit of bad luck. I had only six days in which to work – and no one to work with. I wanted to go to my hotel, but Nechung insisted that we go to Boudhanath. Once there, I attempted to pay for the taxi, but was pressed aside by Nechung, who produced a thick roll of rupee notes and slipped the fee to the driver. We made it a point to begin my visits with some circumambulations of the Boudhanath stupa, but this time we were stopped at the gate by a man in a ticket booth who wanted to charge me 50 rupees to enter. Nechung hustled me over to a side entrance located behind a local market, but as we circled the stupa, I looked suspiciously over my shoulder, expecting to be asked to produce my ticket stub. The thought that admission was being charged at the stupa square, where

I had lived only a few years earlier, was depressing, though I consoled myself that many other sacred places also charged admission (such as Westminster Abbey in London, Teotihuacan in Mexico City, and the Taj Mahal in Agra). Struggling to orient myself to mounting disappointment, I was led by Nechung along a dark, muddy road and into a cluster of houses that I recognized as Arubari from my previous work in the area. Nechung opened the door and welcomed me into a simple room furnished with a few chairs, two bedrolls on the damp cement floor, and in the middle an open suitcase with clothes spilling out. He flung my bag beside it and led me, confused, into an adjacent living area, which was crowded with many of the people who had greeted me at the airport.

Once inside we began to talk, as Maya and several of the other women huddled over a propane stove to make me an omelette. I asked Nechung why we had come to this place rather than his factory in Jorpati. He explained that he was in arrears on his rent and that the landlord had padlocked the building with all of his belongings inside: carpet looms, tools, furniture, personal items, and even the family's clothes, except what they were able to take in the suitcase. He explained that carpet orders had fallen off a few years before, that he was reduced to weaving stock, often taking less for his finished work than it had cost to make – eating loss, as it were, in hopes that the situation would turn around in the near future. But redemption had never arrived. In addition to the loss of his son two years earlier, now the material basis for his family was taken from him and he was living on charity. I was angered by the landlord's actions and reflected that a Canadian landlord could not act in a similar manner. Legal recourse ought to be possible, I suggested. But what were Nepal's laws to Nechung? Regardless of his legal rights to his own property, Nechung was alienated from those rights by his own perception that Nepal's laws were not for people like him.

In a state of indignation, I offered to help. How much did he owe? Two and a half lakh rupees. Referring to a foreign exchange receipt form that I had in my pocket from the airport, I calculated this to be nearly $4,000 CAD. I was astonished that a landlord would allow such a debt to amass, but knew then that I did not have the resources to pay this amount for him, neither with me nor in the near future. I told him so and the anticipation in his eyes withered. I tried to explain that we had a new house, a new baby, and that I was in debt myself. I was not declining to help, I simply did not have the resources to do so.

Perhaps if I had had the kind of money needed at the time, I would have given it without question, but my inability to pay relieved me from having to confront lingering doubts about how the money would be spent or how the debt had been incurred in the first place. This was a contradictory response to our shared history, throughout which I had strived to maintain a distinction between personal reciprocation and a reluctance to become tangled in commercial matters. Nechung had consistently tried to involve me in business ventures by encouraging me to get into carpet exports. We did experiment with some sample carpets and special orders as "fair trade" products, which I sold to friends and family, but I always cautioned him that I was no businessman and had little trust in the cold calculations of capitalism. He may not have accepted this response at first – I was after all the foreigner who was key to the promise of higher status and prosperity that earlier he had said "was written in his head." But now he finally saw that what was written was not what he had hoped for.

I attempted to recover by offering to speak with the landlord, arguing that Nechung should at least be allowed his tools and personal belongings so that he could get back to work and end his humiliation. Nechung quietly, fatalistically, said that there was no point, a sentiment echoed by the others in the room. Maya placed the cooked omelette in front of me, gesturing with her hand to please eat.

Later that week, just before I was to return to Canada, Nechung, Maya, and their surviving son, Dawa, joined me at Shyam's house in Lazimpat for a meal, prepared by Shyam's wife, Anuparma. Nechung and his family looked uncomfortable in comparatively affluent Lazimpat, a new suburb a few blocks away from the Narayanhiti Palace in which the new king, Gyanendra, was holding court and weighing his options. We ate our dal bhaat solemnly. Nechung announced that he would go to work with a friend in India, as there was no work in Nepal, and asked me to escort him to the bus park afterwards for his departure. Nechung asked Anuparma about Shyam, who had left for the United States a year earlier and was working at a liquor store and remitting money back to Nepal so that they could build their own home. Nechung smiled; it is better without a landlord, he remarked.

After the meal, we stepped out onto the narrow porch for a cigarette. Nechung took a draw, and asked if it was possible to come to Canada, to work in Canada. If Shyam could do so well in the United States, he thought, why couldn't he do the same in Canada? The same sense of helplessness that had overcome me a few days earlier returned. I knew how unlikely it was that the Canadian Embassy in New Delhi would issue a visa to someone like Nechung, particularly now that his bank account had been emptied to send Phulmaya to Dubai. With no assets, no employment, and a family spread across three countries, it was almost certain that a visa application would be rejected. I pointed out to Nechung that he spoke neither English nor French. "I could learn," he said. "It would only take me a few days." I told him that it would be unlikely that a visa would be granted to him. "But you could write me a letter. You could sponsor me," he pleaded. I replied that I could write a letter, but that it would not be enough. I knew this from experience, having on numerous occasions been asked to sponsor people to migrate to Canada. I had written letters for some of them, but none was successful. Visas for the West were notoriously difficult to obtain even for educated Nepalese who spoke English fluently; one Tibetan exporter told me that he had been repeatedly denied a visa to travel to the USA for business, even though he owned a large and successful enterprise that he would not likely abandon for the opportunity of, say, working in a liquor store. Given these barriers, it seemed very cruel to encourage hopeless possibilities. We butted our cigarettes and went back inside to collect his suitcase.

I hailed a taxi and we all climbed in and drove to the tourist ghetto at Thamel, from which the bus to India was leaving. I had with me a number of US dollars in traveller's cheques that I was not likely to use, so I changed it into Indian rupees for Nechung, who reluctantly took it. It was not the two and a half lakh rupees he needed to reopen his factory or a visa and passage to Canada, but it was something, something that seemed a pittance in comparison with all of the sorrow and humiliation he had suffered. I felt ashamed as I handed him the money, as this was all that I could now muster in repayment for the generosity with which he had included me in his life over the past seven years. Around us the occasional tourist ambled by in the shallow mud, fending off vendors desperate to sell muscle balm, cheap khukri knives, and plastic Buddhas. Nechung wordlessly embraced me, picked up his case, and walked towards his bus, followed by his family. I couldn't bear to look any further, turned, and walked back to Lazimpat in the rain, heartbroken.

Like all anthropologists I had received training in research ethics, though on reflection it had ill prepared me for the day-to-day choices that had to be made when doing fieldwork. All the case studies used to think through ethical research in the field were based on situations in which ethical boundaries were delineated in broad strokes: stolen goods as "gifts," inside knowledge about criminal activity, infants abandoned in fields by desperate parents. Instutitional research ethics guidelines, national standards (in Canada contained in the *Tri-Council Policy Statement: Ethical Conduct for Research Involving Humans*), and disciplinary guidelines such as those for the American Anthropological Association emphasize professional ethical standards that overshadow consideration of an orientation towards a personal ethic. What is right or what is wrong? What is benign and what is harmful?

To an extent, the codification of research ethics over the past twenty years in Canada, the USA, and Europe has reduced research ethics training to the mastery of bureaucratic procedures, which alienates many anthropologists, who chafe under the "creep" of biomedical standards misapplied to other research paradigms (Haggerty 2004). In Canada, for example, the 1998 *Tri-Council Policy Statement* (revised in 2010) imposed a regime of institutional oversight that every student or faculty researcher working at a Canadian university or college must submit to. Even though most of the research I conducted in 1998 and earlier was not vetted through that regime, the *Tri-Council Policy Statement* contains principles and practices that best represent the ethical guidelines that framed my work from the outset. According to it, if research places participants at greater risk of physical, social, or psychological harm than they would encounter in everyday life, the researcher must weigh favourably the social benefit of the knowledge they create against this potential harm to the participant. This principle is drawn directly from medical research – a guideline, for example, for testing medical treatments – but its application to the social sciences, and anthropological ethnography in particular, creates considerable friction with some of the fundamental assumptions of the discipline.

Fieldwork is conducted in everyday life. At the same time, the presence of the researcher alters the everyday lives of research participants; things cannot be as they were before an interloper arrives with nothing more to contribute to a life than to observe it. Unlike other disciplines in which research tends to be a discrete activity cloistered from the everyday in laboratories or statistical abstractions, ethnography brings us face to face with that life. Even though there may be no intention of putting other people at risk, our mere presence in their lives may have that effect. To the extent that we can, we protect them by maintaining confidentiality and ensuring their anonymity so that we do not expose them to harmful outsiders, who may exploit or oppress them because of what they reveal to us. But such discretion does little to protect them from the harmful, subtle changes that are the unintended, unanticipated, and inevitable consequence of our face-to-face presence in their lives. The casual suggestion, a promise, a gift given, an opinion uttered, an appeal declined, or an offer accepted – all are practices that characterize the give and take of everyday life, and their effect is amplified by an ethnographic encounter across substantial social distances.

The non-dynamic manner in which these social distances are conceptualized by research ethics regimes do not square with my experiences as an ethnographer. As discursive subjects of protected dignity, participants are apt to be cast in the paternalistic model as recipients of our ethical planning and procedures. It is we researchers who are charged with the capacity and responsibility to ameliorate the effects of power on our encounters with others. In the give and take of everyday life, however, we frequently find that this capacity is inadequate in the face of other capacities; that is, others have their own ideas on the sort of demands we ought to make on one another. My relationship with Nechung, for example, was subject not only to my considerations, but to his as well. I was not in a sole position to define and evaluate my relationship with Nechung in anticipation of every possible harm that might befall him. The ongoing transactions of our relationship were as much in his hands as in my own.

In a sense, they were even more so. With limited linguistic and cultural competence in the field, most ethnographers have to take their cues from the others with whom they work, and thus our ability to anticipate these everyday transactions is limited. I relied on Nechung (and others) to orient my way through the world of carpet weavers, saahuji, exporters, and subcontractors. In Uttar Bhanjyang he presided over my introduction to the community of lamas (both Yolmo and Tamang), and I trusted him to negotiate everyday interactions. Had I been alone or if my knowledge of these contexts been mediated by another man (or woman) who occupied a different social space than Nechung did, my relationship with and understanding of Boudhanath and Uttar Bhanjyang would not be as it is now. Nechung, moreover, also protected me from the anticipated harm that these places posed, at least as he understood them. His warning about Tsering Lama's influence after the paati ceremony is one example.

However, the tragic developments in Nechung's life immediately after the ceremony beg the question as to whether my presence in his world affected those events and required some intervention on my part. Not that I should have somehow anticipated the collapse of the carpet industry, or Pruba's untimely death, but that I should have responded to them differently than I did. Nechung simply tried to soldier on as before, maintaining his factory and a son in a Tibetan school in India despite mounting debts. I understood this course, recalling that Nechung had worked in the carpet industry continuously from the age of twelve and did not know of any alternative that would not reduce him to subsistence farming and bearing loads, a life he seemed keen to leave behind and that he could not bring himself to return to. I should have helped him more, financially, at the time, but doing so was really beyond my power.

Perhaps I also could have not allowed my entanglement with Nechung and his family to tighten as it did. The donation to the paati, carpet models co-designed and purchased, further occasional financial assistance, numerous letters, email, and telephone calls (at some expense, particularly for Nechung) drew our lives uncomfortably close. Although his suffering occurred at a distance, it affected me profoundly even if not directly. I could have placed clearer boundaries around our relationship, allowing for analytic distance from Nechung and his family. But I did not. However, this choice was not my own to make. It was Nechung who arrived at my flat one day with the gift of a carpet, and it was Nechung who transformed my offer to donate to a local construction project into a much more ambitious one in Uttar Bhanjyang. Though it was the shared interest in my research that made these actions possible, I did not initiate either as part of a strategy to increase access to research data. The carpet was an unexpected gift, and the paati donation was conceived originally as a gift of gratitude for access already granted. These gifts and the continued bonds between Nechung, Phulmaya, and me grew out of a research encounter but became more than that, and it would have been a misuse of my capacity and responsibility to turn them away. This choice could have been personal, as opposed to professional, but it is not one that I would have ever wanted to make.

A thornier ethical problem to consider is what social benefit my relationship with Nechung and his family has had. An adage of biomedical research that has been explicitly integrated into most research ethic guidelines is that new knowledge, once constructed, must be put to some (therapeutic) use. What my research with Nechung revealed, more than anything else, was the effect of global inequality. His life, career, and circumstance are affected by the capriciousness of the global oriental carpet market; he rode its spectacular rise to small-scale entrepreneurial success and now followed its decline, losing the modest gains he had made – and more – in the process. How can my account contribute to the re-imagination of this inequality or to ameliorating its effects? If there is a therapy for global inequality it is beyond my means to prescribe it, and it would be disingenuous to propose a remedy that I think academic anthropologists are powerless to put into effect. All that I can offer here is to witness the suffering and to convey it as best I can to a reader who, I hope, will recognize that I shared it in small part even if, like a dog biting the hand that feeds it, I owe my own life, career, and circumstance to the same structural inequalities that I am bound, by my profession, to oppose.

Nechung continued to write to me on a regular basis from India. Rather, he continued to dictate his messages to me to a local ghostwriter, so that there was always an added level of interpretation in everything I received from him. The Indian letters were postmarked from Himachal Pradesh and the quality of ghostwriting was somewhat diminished from what was available in Kathmandu. In them, the English language was so distorted that I could not understand some of the letters except at a most superficial level. One letter included a snapshot of Nechung standing in front of the quarry where he was employed, holding a tumpline for a bamboo basket. Another man standing beside him bore a similar tumpline across his forehead, the basket hanging on his back. The baskets struck me as similar to the *doko* baskets worn by porters in the Nepalese hills, though here they no doubt functioned to move gravel and stone from one place to another. Back-breaking manual labour, the historical burden of the Tamang. Nechung's letters, or what I could understand from them, were stoical, but the sadness and humiliation of his new life was a constant subtext.

That humiliation was even more painful because Nechung's fall was so public. The successful entrepreneur and community benefactor was now a labourer once again, having lost everything in the struggle to maintain his stature. As if needing to hide his shame from his fellow villagers, he chose to go to India to suffer this humiliation, even though he stated to me repeatedly in his letters that he was compelled to go to

India, as there was no work in Nepal. Many of his fellow villagers continued to struggle in Kathmandu, and some even weathered the global downturn in the carpet industry and remained in business. When I caught up with Phulmaya two years later, she told me that her father's business had failed because he could not get any credit from his friends, having been unable to repay them in the past. The weavers – the skilled carpet weavers whom he had carefully cultivated in the past – had either moved on to more stable employment or returned to Uttar Bhanjyang to keep their fields when living in Kathmandu was no longer viable. The chöten that we built together, a symbol of Nechung's wealth and influence only five years earlier, was now a crumbling monument to the impermanence of his aspiration. The trail to Uttar Bhanjyang, and beyond, is littered with many more of them.

However, to say that Nechung's migration to India was a choice is not to diminish the structural conditions that conspired against him, that made his flight a path of least resistance. All of the influence that he had accumulated in the village – the partnerships, alliances, and implicit understandings – were of little use as he tried to adapt to a changing field of action that he was thrust onto: the globalized carpet industry. Knowing how to adapt to shifting market conditions, understanding Western consumer tastes, and being able to communicate across cultures were the kind of skills that this new economy demanded. Nechung's initial successes were as a subcontractor and craftsman, but they could not carry him any further to the heights that he imagined for himself. Even though he was a semi-literate lama from Helambu, he was nevertheless aware that sustained, autonomous success would require a new kind of literacy that could lead to fruitful global connections. Nechung deployed the tools at hand, limited though they were, to develop those connections – and I was the object of that deployment.

By pursuing my collaboration with Nechung, I had blundered into a cycle of gift giving and expectation of return. Nechung was at first a research participant, then a friend, then a partner in an enterprise in which my participation was key. From our first tentative gestures of reciprocity – giving cigarettes, cups of tea, bottles of soda, carpets – our lives became more and more entangled, so that we now shared Nechung's failure. But where my role was mostly to try to understand it, he was forced to live it. Nechung exemplified for me a Yolmo petty entrepreneur struggling valiantly in a global economy; to Nechung, I exemplified a *bidhesi* (foreigner) who had access to resources that had made him a big man in the past and could be drawn on to do so in the future. This double subjection, mutual Othering, led us both to disappointment. For despite my initial hope to find in Nechung not only a research subject, but also an equal, a friend, our relationship so far had only reproduced the structural inequalities that forced us further apart.

Chapter Seven

A Family Problem

"Tom-uncle, my father and mother have some kind of problem," Phulmaya told me over the telephone from Dubai in the winter of 2003. The line was crystal clear even though it stretched across ten time zones, so clear that her voice was instantly familiar, as if she were in the next room. Her call was unanticipated, though not unexpected, and her casual tone was a result of her struggle with another language, which belied the gravity of the situation. A letter had arrived from India only a few days before. Maya, Phulmaya's mother and Nechung's wife, had died while in childbirth. In that letter Nechung included a photograph of himself looking expressionlessly into the distance with an infant huddled to his chest. He was far from home and told me that he needed to return to Uttar Bhanjyang as soon as possible to perform the necessary puja. His family was by that time spread out across much of Asia – he was in Himachal Pradesh, two sons were in Bylakkuppe, near Mysore in the south, and Phulmaya was in Dubai. The fact of Maya's death resonated across a continent and further. Nechung's mounting misfortunes weighed heavily on me as well. Nechung and Phulmaya's appeals for help, whether voiced directly or implicit in the detail of their pain, begged the question of my culpability in their condition. What could, or should, I do?

Phulmaya was returning to be with her father. Even though she had been in Dubai for two years, their household continued to exist, connected through a virtual world of email and electronic bank transfers. Its current physical distance was in fact the basis of its existence, as the money she sent home to her father – in the end, 2 lakh rupees – was intended to subsidize the payment of debt, investment in a new carpet factory, and the family's reunion in Kathmandu.

Now that would not happen as planned. I asked Phulmaya what she was going to do when she returned, as she had been out of the country for three years, had studied only to class eight, and possessed few skills other than childcare and housework. She told me that she did not want to get married, she wanted to work abroad again, this time in a *thulo desh*, a "big country," by which she meant Europe, Japan, or the United States.

She asked, of course, about coming to Canada, and I reiterated that that would be enormously difficult. The only program that admitted foreign domestic workers into Canada required that applicants speak English (or French) and that they have a high level of education. Phulmaya added that she would try to get her school leaving certificate (SLC) on return in preparation for work in a "big country." I offered to help, reasoning that even if she never worked abroad again, her options in Nepal would be enhanced by completing her education. I was going to be in Kathmandu in a few months, I told her, and could hire her as a research assistant for a study on transnational migrant girls like herself. It would be an ideal arrangement, I thought. Phulmaya's grasp of English was by no means perfect, but it complemented my own imperfect Nepali. Moreover, her intimate knowledge of the subject would be a useful advantage, as would her close cultural and class proximity to the women I would likely be interviewing. My plan to hire a student from the university there worried me, as they would likely be Brahmin, Chetris, or Newar middle class and thus would have little in common with the women I wanted to interview. I would have my interviews and Phulmaya would have a substantial sum of money that she could apply to her education, all for two weeks' work.

Phulmaya enthusiastically accepted my proposal. At the time it was the most that I could manage financially, and I hoped this would in some small way resolve the tension between my role as a professional anthropologist and my being a member of Nechung's aaphno maanchhe. Despite this intention, or perhaps because of it, I found that the delineation of these roles became blurred as I became complicit in Phulmaya's desperate and somewhat illegitimate effort to achieve her own goals, which, in the face of the constant constraints that she and her family faced because of their providence and social class, now appeared entirely reasonable.

Pierre Bourdieu (1998, 65) once wrote that family is a "world in which the ordinary laws of the market are suspended," a world he described by Aristotle's term "philia," which indicates "a refusal to calculate," distinguishing family relations, bound by rules of generalized reciprocity and affect, from friendship. He added that the "family discourse" that shapes our conception and practice of that institution obscures its role as a site of capital accumulation and social reproduction. Family members have always had an inherent or acquired value and a role in the household economy that precedes family affect. Children, in particular, are assets. Though children have been described as liabilities in the modern context, in that they are materially unproductive and need to be nourished and cared for, they represent a potential that can increase the capital stock of a family if by "family" we mean more than a unit of related individuals, an intergenerational patrimony that provides a basis for future generations. In the past few years Phulmaya had become one of the most important assets in her family. Indeed its very future and survival depended on her.

Her reference to me over the telephone as "Tom-uncle" was an endearing but not a benign honour. Over the years, the children of many of my friends and co-workers in Nepal addressed me as "uncle," reversing the English language order of the honorific; of course, I was not really their uncle, but still accrued all of the rights and obligations that go with that title. In the case of Phulmaya, I knew that I was expected to help. It would be a considerable breach of a shared expectation if I did not, though I was not clear about what Phulmaya or Nechung expected. My fictive membership in this family put real claims on me and I was apprehensive about how my response would be interpreted.

I wanted to help Phulmaya, but I also had needs. Ethnographic research is often a pragmatic entanglement of these and similar motivations. Any "professionalism" that draws a rigid boundary between the personal and the business of conducting research, not only makes ethnography difficult to do, but subjects the all too human facework of relationship making to abstract, and ultimately arbitrary, rules of protocol. Not only were Phulmaya and Nechung unaware of the rules I was working under, but they had their own implicit set of rules that I was expected to learn and follow.

The Maoist insurgency raged in the hills all around Kathmandu in the summer of 2003. As my taxi sped from the airport, it passed a heavily armed military checkpoint. There were no garlands, no silk khatas, to welcome me to Nepal this time, just a 50-calibre machine gun surrounded by sandbags and razor wire. The taxi headed into the centre of the city, leaving behind muddy and potholed roads; crawled gradually

A Family Problem

onto the broad, freshly paved avenue in front of the Narayanhiti palace; turned at a newly installed traffic light that marked the brightly painted intersection across from the American club; and stopped at a hotel in Lazimpat. I entered and registered. In the past, I had frequently been met at the airport by Nechung, Shyam, or other friends and then whisked directly to Boudhanath, where we feasted on fresh momo in the joy of reunion. This time I arrived alone, anonymous, and ate a nondescript plate of fried rice in view of a wooden watchtower where bored soldiers stared out at the street from inside the palace compound.

I phoned Nechung, who was staying with friends in Jorpati. We spoke briefly and nervously and arranged to meet the next day at the hotel. Though exhausted from the flight and two lengthy layovers in London and Abu Dhabi, I was restless and walked, breathing in air perfumed with incense and gasoline fumes. I passed the gleaming, regal UNICEF office in Lainchaur and, on the other side of the street, noticed fresh plasterwork on the government dairy outlet where we often used to buy coconut yogurt. Earlier that year the Maoists had bombed the dairy outlet in plain view of the Narayanhiti palace. Yogurt had been deemed an affront to the revolution and its delectableness was of no concern to those attacking the means of production. A patrol of heavily armed, camouflaged soldiers snaked down the sidewalk. I purchased a cheroot from a roadside vendor and retreated to smoke it in my room, trying to numb myself by watching a program on Star TV. The power went out after about twenty minutes, owing to load shedding, so I slept.

The next morning the streets had been washed by an early monsoon shower. I strolled along the road outside the British Embassy compound to shake my sadness at the changes I was seeing. Behind the high, whitewashed walls, towering chir pines cast shade onto the treeless street. A sign posted on a door read in English, "Please no refuse." Directly below the sign lay a midden of discarded plastic bags full of garbage being rummaged through by two or three young ragpickers, barefoot children dressed in tattered shirts and shorts brandishing hooked, sharpened steel rods to probe the bags, looking for anything to salvage. Sitting to one side was another small group of boys inhaling solvents from the same orange plastic bags that lay on the ground. A few others lay prostrate in the shade. I was used to ragpickers, to children crippled by polio with their hands outstretched, to menacing groups of boys at political demonstrations, but this was the first time in twelve years that I had observed such a pathetic scene. That such

Figure 7.1. Communist Party student union demonstration outside the Indian Embassy, July 2003.

desperation was going on a few hundred metres from both the palace and the UNICEF office with its gilded, gated entrance was an irony that only intensified my horror. I quickened my pace and returned to the hotel.

Nechung and Phulmaya arrived later in the morning and we sat in the spartan hotel lobby to talk. I ordered soft drinks and offered Nechung an Indian-made cigarette, much as he had done when we first met eight years earlier. He declined, saying that he had quit smoking, but the refusal had little effect on our conversation. We had not seen each other since 2001, when I had made a brief visit that was truncated, owing to the assassination of the former king, and there was much to catch up on. Nechung told me that he had started a new carpet factory in Boudhanath and was getting a few orders from exporters. "The carpet business is very hard," he said, and I knew that small, independent manufacturers like him were struggling across the Kathmandu valley.

However, carpet making was all that he knew, having been raised and educated in the factories. His options were limited.

I turned to Phulmaya and spoke about my plans to interview about ten former transnational domestic workers. I went over some of the ethical concerns about what I planned to do, as Phulmaya and most of the women I wanted to speak to had been, in a sense, "trafficked" to the Persian Gulf to evade the authorities. Prior to 2003 it was illegal for unmarried Nepalese women to work abroad. While many thousands of males joined a burgeoning exodus of young workers to Saudi Arabia, Kuwait, the United Arab Emirates, and Bahrain, young women who were in demand as domestic servants in the same countries remained under the protective authority of their fathers and husbands, while women from India, Sri Lanka, and the Philippines travelled freely (Graner 2003; Shah and Menon 1999). The discriminatory nature of this policy was vociferously pointed out by Nepalese feminists, but was obscured, ultimately, by a widespread moral panic about the conflation of domestic labour with prostitution and about the vulnerability of young women to physical and sexual abuse while abroad.

While women travelling out of the country by air were closely monitored at Nepal's one international airport, the officially open border with India was a frontier that was more difficult to police, and it was across this border that thousands of Nepalese girls were trafficked into Mumbai's notorious sex trade. Many of those girls came from the Sindhupalchok region, specifically from several villages near Uttar Bhanjyang, so that most female migration from the area was suspected of being involved in prostitution. A journalist once charged that every home in the region that was roofed with tin, rather than from traditional materials such as slate or wooden shake, was in fact the home of a family who had a daughter in the sex trade, ignoring the contributions of those who worked in the carpet industry, or in India, or like Phulmaya in the Persian Gulf and who were sending remittances home. Alarmingly then, all signs of personal economic affluence in the area were judged by many in the media and in international NGOs to be indications of living off the profits of prostitution.

In order to get work in the Persian Gulf prior to 2003, a substantial number of young women, like Phulmaya, were forced to travel to India, from where they could fly out to the Persian Gulf unimpeded by Nepalese immigration officials., Clandestine networks of brokers, middlemen, and corrupt government officials cooperated to secretly convey these girls to the Gulf, charging the families who sent them for the service. This secrecy aroused suspicions of sex trade subterfuge, of luring girls into prostitution on the pretext of getting lucrative jobs in the Persian Gulf. Ironically, these suspicions were reinforced by the same measures intended to protect women from prostitution and abuse, forcing the networks underground.

Neither Phulmaya nor Nechung had any qualms about how she got there, and both seemed oblivious to the purported risks and to the reputation attending female migration. For them, the benefits outweighed the risks. As Nechung's factory fell further and further into debt, the promise of remittances wired electronically into bank accounts was palpable. "I am sending my daughter to Kuwait," he declared in a letter before the first of Phulmaya's two foreign contracts as a domestic worker. Phulmaya, for her part, appeared only too happy to travel abroad to help her struggling family. Though no longer a child in a formal sense, as an unmarried daughter she was still attached to her father's household. I had always found it interesting that Phulmaya did not weave carpets, even though carpet weaving was going on all around her. I didn't know whether this was intentional or accidental. The domestic work she had learned assisting her mother with her two younger brothers was the only marketable skill she had. Now there was an international market for those skills and compelling reasons for her and her family to ignore the legal restrictions on that market.

Phulmaya seemed enthusiastic about the project, not only because of the money that she would earn, but also because of the attention it focused on her and her expertise, similar to the attention her father had received from me in the past. Nechung sat silently. Phulmaya then began to tell me of the pleasant time she had had in Dubai, how she much preferred it to Kuwait, when an anguished howl broke through her cheerfully composed smile, as if a terrible thought had been forced through. Tears flowed down, flooding her speech. She seemed to gasp for a few moments and then cried, "I miss my mother!" Nechung blinked and avoided my gaze, betraying no emotion. I filled the pained silence with some platitude that even then seemed inadequate to the situation. Phulmaya wiped her eyes, "I am sorry, I am sorry ..." she muttered, as if expressions of grief were allowed only if scripted, only if they were placed in the proper container. That Maya's death occurred at a time of family dislocation only compounded the tragedy. Recalling Dubai triggered the painful memory and it weighed on us in the hotel lobby. Eventually, the conversation regained its momentum, but I became more reticent as I began to sense that I was intruding upon some deeply private suffering.

Family is a place where we intimately share pain, loss, and regret before disclosing them to the world outside. This is because family is conceived of as a space, though not necessarily a physical space, that is sacred and thus separate from the secular public sphere, where its members are sheltered from the calculation of others. The family as a domestic space is dominated by men, but its thresholds are defined and defended by women, who labour to recreate what Pierre Bourdieu (1998, 68) called the bonds of "affective obligations and obligated affections" that produce the effect of family solidarity. It is women who play a primary role in monitoring how family members interrelate, exchange both material and emotional "goods" with one another, and observe day-to-day religious and cultural rituals.

The sentimental view of the family as a sacred space in which members are sustained and protected from outsiders does not take into account how families function as economic units in which the accumulation of capital, in all of its forms, threatens them with dissolution. Families fail because of tensions introduced by competing material interests. It was not uncommon for me to hear of individual members of Nepalese families, for example, who were *chuteko*, cut off from the rest because of tensions around money, inheritance, or marital choice. By turning their backs on the affective obligations that compose the family as an institution, these individuals paid a heavy emotional cost.

Thinking of family in this way has helped me to understand the trepidation I had, and continue to have, about the fictive kinship relationships that were commonly proffered by research participants. Casual acquaintances, people I had barely met, often referred to me as "uncle," or to my wife as "aunt" (always using the English words), trying to insinuate us into their family networks. These efforts often struck me as somewhat less than sincere, though I knew that they were modelled on numerous Nepali-*bidhesi* relationships with tourists, NGO workers, and researchers that appeared to be successful – and lucrative – for others. The failure of these efforts to build relationships with powerful outsiders is a result of a miscalculation of the strength of those relationships; for while affective obligations may be in force within families and, to an extent, broader kinship groups, they weaken with distance. Hearing myself described as fictive kin by relative strangers struck me as a cynical attempt to coerce resources, even though the socioeconomic disparities that motivated those attempts were undeniable.

I do not blame them for trying.

I never felt that Phulmaya's almost playful definition of me as an "uncle" was a tactical appeal to an affective obligation, probably because I had known her for almost eight years by that point. But it was. The compulsion of that obligation was ever present, a sense that ours was a balanced reciprocity that implied that we had expectations of each other. Fictive kinship is ambiguous in that the obligations that lie, implicitly, between people are known to be fictitious, already demystified. The force of these obligations is a complex cultural problem; when one gives assistance or a gift, how soon afterwards is a return expected? What is an appropriate value for that returned gift or service?

This reduction of family relationships, even fictive ones, to economic reckoning would seem to most of us in the (post-) industrial north a violent intrusion of the social into the sacred, into a realm that is ideally beyond calculation. I doubt, though, that a similar logic holds in urban lama families, which are only recent and partial converts to the domesticity that characterized families before the women's movement and the rise of female participation in the workforce. Lama families and households continue to be productive institutions, allocating family labour and resources in a corporate fashion with the expectation that all of its members will conform to its sustainability or, more hopefully, its upward mobility. Nechung's statement that he was sending Phulmaya to Kuwait is but one example of how he, like most lama men, control or are expected to control their ummarried daughter's labour, just as they control or are expected to control their exchange in marriage.

Fictive kinship has also been described as a way to control labour resources. The classic ethnographic example of *compradazgo* in Latin America, in which godparents deploy the labour of their godchildren as compensation for their patronage, is a good example. Fictive kinship conforms with Bourdieu's conception of family as a "field," rather than a "body." Some may argue that I was exploiting my relationship with Nechung and Phulmaya in order to advance my own interest in accumulating research data. But Nechung and Phulmaya were also calculating what would be gained in return, as they also calculated each other's contributions. Bourdieu's notion of family as field is useful in that it unmasks the common sense to reveal the instrumental mechanisms that structure our relationships, but this business of extracting and subordinating affective motivations from instrumental ones strikes me as reductive. The isolation of specific elements of social phenomena so that they might be better described in relation to others is a fundamental methodology for many ethnographers and was especially so for Bourdieu. But to proceed as if the instrumental drives the affective is to make instrumental motivation an enemy of affection, where in my view they are better understood as partners in a fragile embrace. Our affections enable these mechanisms, they make them possible in the first place, even if they are materially transformed by them. This is particularly true of lama families in the first decade of the twenty-first century as they combined resources to subsist and persist collectively.

Similarly, it is not so easy to conceptually separate the instrumental and affective aspects of my relationship with Phulmaya and Nechung; indeed it would denigrate the complex dynamic of any relationship to attempt to do so. Our relationship is based on fieldwork, because without it there would have been little for us to ground a friendship in, but it is more than that. I have had other fieldwork relationships that have not been sustained in the years after the work was done, but there has been consistent contact with Nechung and his family. What binds us is a willingness to continue to try to make and meet our obligations, even if we occasionally fall short in the eyes of the other.

Outside an internet cafe at Jorpati Chowk, I waited for Phulmaya. Trucks and buses passed, oblivious to the throngs of pedestrians, roadside merchants, and grazing cattle, throwing dust and black smoke into the air. Taxis honked at me, as if offended by my presence. Although not much apparently had changed since my first visit to this place, there seemed to be many more people. A convoy of soldiers passed, moving from their base in Sankhu, where ten years earlier we used to watch them rehearse airborne tactics, their parachutes drifting lazily to the ground behind the trees of the royal forest. Then, Nepal's martial traditions were safely confined to the training fields; now it had spilled into the streets. I watched a pathetic looking policeman, armed with only a bamboo lathi, adjust his face mask.

Phulmaya appeared out of the crowd to lead me to Nechung's shared flat in Jorpati, a stone's throw away from the factory that he had lost two years earlier. She was in better spirits than on the day before. I was struck by the fact that the shy young girl I had barely made out as a family member in 1995 was now an articulate, cosmopolitan young woman dressed in fashionably branded denim jeans, not in the cheap Chinese imports available at the market in Boudhanath or in the drab Tibetan dress smeared with grease and charcoal that had been her sole garment when she lived with her mother and father. We stopped briefly outside the internet cafe while she chatted excitedly with a young woman emerging from inside. "She is emailing her husband," she explained, her voice competing with a quarrel at a nearby fruit stand. "He is working in Malaysia." Phulmaya had an extensive network of friends, most of whom had recently been abroad to Kuwait or Dubai in the United Arab Emirates. Many of her friends were still there, working on a second or third two-year work permit. I was hoping to interview some of these women, but first I was going to conduct the interview with Phulmaya, not only because I was interested her experiences as a migrant domestic worker, but also because this allowed me to test the interview and survey questions that I had written and translated into Nepali before leaving Canada.

Nechung's new quarters consisted of a room and kitchen that he shared with a gregarious landlord and a number of young men and women who crowded around me as I entered. Down a narrow walk was Nechung's new carpet factory, modest but active, and an office bulging with rolls of wool and designs. This is what Phulmaya's remittances had bought – a chance to make a living again from his craft, to not have to bear loads of gravel and stone that weighed also on his identity. After a few minutes, he emerged from his factory and greeted me warmly. A boy was sent to fetch soft drinks. I was anxious to begin the interview, but knew that these informalities were a requisite preamble to any formal work. Nechung's landlady asked what I was doing in Nepal: was I a tourist or was I going trekking? Nechung interrupted, saying that I was a teacher from Canada, who had come to study the carpet industry. I added that I was now actually more interested in studying Nepal's new *lahure*, such as Phulmaya. There was a pause as she stared at Phulmaya. "*Lahure?*" she repeated. She then put a string of questions to Nechung in dialect which I could not follow. Phulmaya joined in what appeared to be an animated debate. In a lull in the conversation, she reported to me in halting English that the landlady was confused, because she understood *lahure* to refer specifically to those who served in the Gurkha battalions of the British and Indian armies. I had gleaned the term from the Nepali press and from the title of a recent book on Nepali transnational labour by David Seddon, Jaganath Adhikari, and Ganesh Gurung (2001). What I had thought was a vernacular term for the flood of recent migrants going to the Persian

Gulf and South Asia was in fact an academic appropriation of a term that has long referred to Nepal's mercenary exports (*lahure* indicates Lahore, which in British India was the centre for Gurkha recruitment). By implication, migrant labour was seen as both unskilled and dangerous mercenary work and a form of colonial subjugation.

After about an hour of conversation we agreed to begin the interview. Phulmaya and I went into Nechung's room and I began to set up the tape recorder and organize the questions. I was somewhat surprised when Nechung followed us in and sat at the side of the room to observe. This posed an awkward dilemma. I wanted to hear Phulmaya's perspective, but having her father in the room might lead to her being less than forthcoming on some key questions I wanted to ask. It was, after all, Nechung's room. In the end I made the spontaneous decision not to ask him to leave, a decision based more on intuition than considered reasoning. Fieldwork often does not afford us the time to reasonably consider our actions, it is often an improvised, not a scripted, performance. As a result, the interview I translated addressed Phulmaya's articulation of her obligations and her sacrifice in service of her family's welfare, rather than an individual account of her experiences in the Gulf.

As always, there was a struggle with language, dialect, and noise. The concrete walls of Nechung's room seemed to amplify the racket outside just as it absorbed what was said inside, and the microphone could not overcome these limitations. But this retrospective scripting of the interview shows it to be a triangular discussion that also amplified the emphasis placed on family problems and resulted in Phulmaya's evasive answer to my most pressing question. The decision to go to Kuwait was not taken by her alone; it was a family affair. Later in the interview, she spoke of the comparatively large outlay of money – her father's money – that was required to arrange for the work visa and travel arrangements to Kuwait, paid out to clandestine and somewhat disreputable networks of agents, middlemen, and corrupt employers. One important aspect of the interview protocol was that participants were asked not to divulge the identity of any of these people, because of the remote possibility that the information could be used to incriminate them at a later date.

This context exposed the naiveté of the original question. Individual decisions are always embedded in family, kin, and group consideration, particularly among the people I was working with. However, there has been a consistent theme in much ethnography on transnational migration that suggests that some family members, in particular the women who work abroad as domestic servants, are forced to do so by their desperate, or just greedy, families. One anthropologist, for example, argues that such activity amounts to a "commoditization of the family" in which family relationships are "forcibly reduced to monthly remittances" (Parreñas 2001, 249). I wondered if this was the case for Phulmaya as well, but Nechung's presence in the room led Phulmaya to put the emphasis on family responsibility, not on personal sacrifice.

Phulmaya did speak of her sacrifices as well, though nowhere did she ever admit to the kind of abuse and maltreatment that had become a consistent theme in the Nepalese media. She had in fact abandoned her first two-year contract in Kuwait after only one year, as she worked under very harsh, restrictive conditions looking after fourteen children of various ages, cooking, cleaning, and doing the laundry for the entire household. She cared for these children from early morning until they were in bed. Even if she had had any leisure time, she could not show her face outside the family compound, she could not speak with her "madam's" husband, and she told me, with characteristic understatement, that her "madam" was a "little bit strict or harsh" (*ali ali kaDaa thyo*). Her reticence on this subject, I feared, was also a result of the three-way dynamic, although there was no evidence that anything untoward had happened to her. The only reason to suspect it might be so was that the media and some NGOs were intent on reiterating horror stories about the horrible fate that awaited female migrants in the Persian Gulf or, worse, that such migration was only a cover for the trafficking of women into the Mumbai sex trade.

Phulmaya and the other women that she introduced to me over the next few weeks suggested that the suffering they endured was far less sensational, though compelling nonetheless: isolation, subjection to sometimes racist forms of oppression, overwork, and, above all, separation from their families and the familiarity of their culture, language, and religion. During this time they sent money home to their families, either by post or by electronic bank transfer. In that sense, these migrant women did have something in common with the Gurkha mercenaries who sacrificed and suffered to provide for their families at home (for a discussion of this connection see Seddon, Adhikari, and Gurung 2002). Outsiders draw on this historical analogy of transnational wage labour that is mercenary-like, dirty, difficult, and dangerous. The analogy is one that is imposed on these women, who do not see their sacrifices in such a historical context. Phulmaya and most of the other former migrants described their work as hard, but something that they could and did bear in the best interests of their families. There were few other meaningful options for them, as urban unemployment had grown in recent years and many of them fled Uttar Bhanjyang and Helambu after the Maoists imposed their control over those regions in the past two years. As a young woman, her existing options were further limited to occupations that traditionally drew female labour, such as carpet weaving, but Phulmaya knew full well that weaving would not return the kind of salary that would solve their family's problems. Domestic work was something that she could do, and doing it for such a comparatively high wage abroad fit both the limitations of her gender and the gravity of her family's need.

Phulmaya managed to get a contract to work in Dubai shortly after returning to Kathmandu from Kuwait. In Dubai, she worked in a household that belonged to an expatriate family from India, and she described her working conditions as much better. After the interview, she showed me a photo album from that time: a series of photographs from when she had taken the two children she cared for to a local amusement park, and another series in which she and several Nepalese friends modelled clothes in an impromptu fashion show. Financially, as well, she did much better, remitting 2 lakh rupees to her father, which Nechung used to acquire more carpet-weaving equipment and to rent a new production shed. Now returned from Dubai, Phulmaya was aiming for an even better foreign contract – this time in a thulo desh. Most of the young women that we interviewed later that summer were also searching for new opportunities. Now, like most of them, Phulmaya was looking for herself, not merely to provide for her family.

Some domestic workers from elsewhere who returned after working in the Persian Gulf were able to renegotiate their relationships with parents and spouses from a position of strength (Gamburd 2000). Similarly, becoming a principal breadwinner for the family had refigured Phulmaya's relationship with Nechung. She was no longer a dependent and subordinated child, but was now free to pursue her own interests in addition to providing for her father. In fact, she had managed to put aside about 50,000 rupees for her own use, which she was now living on. With this money in the bank she was in no hurry to find employment and, for a time that summer, her daily routine seemed to revolve around meeting friends and collecting information about future domestic work contracts.

This is where my status as a fictive member of the family came in. After the interview questions were addressed and the interview was officially over, I turned off the tape recorder. As always, it was at this point that some of the most significant conversations took place, communications that were both personal and saturated with data that were useful to my research. Somehow, the personal nature of our discussion made turning off the machine appropriate, so that it was not submitted to the impersonal objectification of recording. On the other hand, much of what was said was so important that I regretted later not having it on tape, despite the violation of privacy that this would have been.

Phulmaya, as her father before her had done, pressed me about coming to Canada. I replied that the situation in Canada was very different, that opportunities for short-term domestic work were few and highly regulated. Where families in many Persian Gulf states receive generous state subsidies to encourage high-fertility rates that made hiring cheap South Asian labour a possibility for those of even a modest income, there was no parallel condition in Canada. Only the extremely wealthy could afford live-in domestic help, and most of that workforce seemed to be coming from the Philippines, a major global provider of domestic labour. She pressed on, arguing that all she would need was a tourist visa. I replied that I was not comfortable sponsoring her for a tourist visa if her intention was to work illegally and that, in any case, it was unlikely that the Canadian Embassy was going to issue a tourist visa to her on my say-so. I knew that a young lama woman stood little chance of being granted a visa, and that any attempt to obtain one from the Canadian consular office in Lazimpat would likely be futile – a waste of time and money.

However, these rationalizations were not all that prevented me from wholeheartedly endorsing Phulmaya's desires. In the back of my mind was the fear that bringing Phulmaya to Canada, even if it were possible, could end badly. I was not comfortable becoming someone who dominated Phulmaya's labour. We preferred that our two-year old daughter attend an organized day care where she would be attended to by strangers who were trained and skilled and received a wage for their service. Day care providers made no additional demands on us couched in metaphors of fictive kinship. I tried as best as I could to lay out these points to Phulmaya and Nechung, but there collided with a significant difference between our conceptions of the family: the modern conception of the family as being beyond calculation, however mystifying and ephemeral, against a conception of the family as a corporate body through which labour is allocated in an explicit form of social calculation. Nechung "sent" his daughter to Kuwait, transforming their relationship in the process, and Phulmaya now expected that I would facilitate her coming to Canada. For much of the rest of our work together that summer I frequently had to reiterate my reluctance to help with this goal, and I feared that my reliance on them both as research associates and as close friends would be jeopardized.

Family was a persistent context and subject for the remaining interviews that Phulmaya helped to facilitate among her friends and relatives from Uttar Bhanjyang. The contradictory interest between families and the young people sent abroad to work did not appear, on the surface at least, to be as much of a problem for Phulmaya and her friends. As Oded Stark (1995) pointed out in his early work on transnational remittance behaviour, pure altruism, as in a child's total subordination to the family's economic need, and pure self-interest are poles of a conceptual continuum that are rarely the case in reality. Family and self-interest are intimately entangled. Our attempt to separate them is grounded in our own conception of families as groups of related individuals who ought to be beyond economic objectification.

Phulmaya's family was not at all like our Western conceptualization of one, nor were those of her friends, an extended circle of women from Uttar Bhanjyang all of whom had worked abroad and were actively searching for more opportunities to do so. Disentangling Phulmaya's interests from Nechung's interests or from the interests of her brothers, both in Nepal and in India, would be like setting the interests of a single organ against the body of which it is a part. Indeed, all my subsequent interviews with Phulmaya's friends were conducted with family members present, in part because of the cramped quarters they lived in, in part because of the novelty of having a foreigner asking questions of one of theirs, and in part, and most important, because of a sense that the matters under discussion were matters for all to hear. The modest accommodations in which the interviews were carried out did not appear impoverished, but they were always teeming with people: children playing, women preparing rice in pressure cookers, and old men smoking and discussing important matters. Open windows were an invitation for passers-by to peer in when they saw a crowd of people huddled around a foreigner.

We met one of Phulmaya's friends, Lakhpa, outside a communications shop in Jorpati, the same place where Phulmaya first found me.

Lakhpa took us back to her flat for the interview, a home that I had passed many times before several years earlier. Two steel shuttered doors on the ground floor were once carpet factories, but now they were empty. She led us up the stairs to the second floor and motioned for us to sit in a well-appointed parlour as she disappeared into the kitchen. She re-emerged several minutes later bearing plates of omlettes, which Phulmaya and I were instructed to eat. Lakhpa's mother followed, carrying plates of snacks. Tea and biscuits followed, carried in by Lakhpa's two sisters, who seemed to appear from out of nowhere as I set the tape recorder to record. From the outset, it was clear that this interview would go well, for Lakhpa had an ability and a desire to express herself in ways that most people from Uttar Bhanjyang that I interviewed could not. In these interviews I probed for information about how they were treated while abroad, looking for and perhaps expecting the sensational – harsh work conditions, abuse, and exploitation. Midway through the interview I asked, "Was there *duhkha* (suffering) when you were in Kuwait?" Lakhpa replied: "No, no. About the work, for me it wasn't hard, and I didn't suffer. Work is work. Sometimes I was sad when I remembered my mother and father; I couldn't meet my mother and father. I didn't suffer because of the work, but I did not see my mother and father for years. Sometimes I got a letter, or we spoke on the phone, and little by little the memories come, and it hurts a little bit." Lakhpa's sisters and mother beamed proudly. Phulmaya audibly agreed, shaking her head in a distinctive figure eight motion.

When I asked Lakhpa if there had been any sadness, regret, or suffering while she worked in Kuwait, I used the Nepali noun *duhkha*. Duhkha can mean sorrow, grief, distress, trouble, problem, or hardship. A Sanskrit word, it is often heard in Nepali or Hindi popular songs that deal with young love thwarted by fate, much as many popular songs in the West do. But the word also has a religious significance that is central to Hinduism and Buddhism, which teach that a fundamental ontological fact of human life is duhkha: suffering, impermanence, and the realization that all life decays into illness, old age, and death. Both meanings resonate in her response, as the sadness of her separation from her family is distinguished from the hardship of labour – a hardship that she denies. A causal connection between Lakhpa's sadness and the fact that her absence is due to her migration is not stated ("work is work"). Without making such a connection in words, she not only subordinates her own hardship to a greater good, but also deems the hardship of labour, and of life, as something that goes without saying, that is, a fact of life that is readily evident and not worthy of remark, particularly when compared with the depth of feeling for her family.

This stoicism seemed to submerge self-regard in favour of familial obligation, but other details in the interviews showed that these young women were working for more than just the family interest. Lakhpa, for example, had remitted about 3 lakh rupees to her family in Jorpati while abroad, and some of that money was used to subsidize her brother's Malaysian work permit, which was organized through one of Kathmandu's many international employment agencies; she also had put aside a sum for her own use. Each of the young women I spoke to did not consider themselves permanently returned to Nepal, as all of them were looking for other opportunities to work abroad, in Korea, the Persian Gulf, or a "big country" such as the United States, Japan, or Europe. Even though the suffering of family separation was palpable, it did not mean that they would be reluctant to be separated again if there was profit to be made. Work is, after all, work, a persistent part of life's condition

After a few days all the interviews had been conducted. One afternoon as I was relaxing with Phulmaya and her father before returning to my hotel, I raised the subject of Phulmaya's education, the plan for her to obtain her School Leaving Certificate (SLC). Whatever illusions that I harboured about the value of an education as an enabling factor that was absent in their lives was countered by their utilitarian view that the SLC would be useful primarily as a much needed credential to work in a "big country." Educational certificates and degrees are in part symbolic, representing the competency and mastery of the holder. All educational credentials are also a kind of fungible cultural capital that, in theory, can be exchanged for higher pay, status, and a passage out of deprivation. But, also in theory, there are no guarantees that such a transaction can be made. Other factors intervene – class, caste, race, gender, and ability – that reinforce barriers, regardless of any credential. Phulmaya was not about to proudly hang her SLC on a wall, but it just might have been useful in obtaining a work visa abroad. I had hoped that by gaining the mastery that an SLC represents, other options and opportunities would be opened for Phulmaya, despite those barriers.

Though SLCs may seem a routine academic credential by Canadian standards – they approximate, roughly, passage from a Canadian middle school – they are notoriously difficult for Nepalese students to obtain. The tests are taken almost a full year after a student finishes formal schooling and candidates often have to hire private tutors to adequately prepare. Owing to those factors, the failure rate of the SLC is quite high and candidates without the financial means to prepare are particularly disadvantaged. As is consistent with educational systems elsewhere, income is a primary indicator in academic success in Nepal. This is where I wanted to help in Phulmaya's case, so I asked how she would go about preparing for the exam. Both Nechung and his daughter looked confused. "An SLC costs 18,000 rupees," Nechung stated flatly. "You mean that is what the tuition costs?" I queried. "Tuition? No, we have the SLC. Now she can go to a big country, like America or Canada." I was not sure I understood the reply or what it implied. What did Nechung and Phulmaya mean that they had the SLC? Did they possess a notarized certificate proclaiming her educational credentials, obtained without her ever qualifying for those credentials, or was the subject of the SLC being dismissed as irrelevant? Phulmaya apparently was not dreaming of attending college or working in an office or an NGO, even though I felt that she could do so if she wanted. In hindsight these expectations are revealed as naïve and ill conceived in the conviction that education could be a panacea for Nechung's and Phulmaya's desperate condition. That was clearly my conviction, not Phulmaya's. Her sights were set on working in a "big country" and having an SLC was instrumental only for obtaining an even more important credential, a visa that would allow this work.

The only thing I was clear about through this exchange was that Phulmaya was not going to use her salary to study for her SLC. I was disappointed, though once again this is a response I now regret, as I ought to have had no expectation of what Phulmaya did after her employment was ended. This was an encounter that betrayed the palpable difference between me and my Nepalese friends, my fictive family. After all, I was using them to obtain data, to augment my cultural capital, get tenure, and become a successful anthropologist. Why shouldn't they attempt the same? Family members do this to each other all the time. The sentimental "family discourse" that informs much ethnography on transnationalism treats families as institutions that are, or ought to be, sacred and beyond calculation. However, families have always been sites of production of all forms of capital. This encounter revealed the fiction of my membership in this family, not because I was objectified as a provider of means, but because I failed, indeed had no way, to provide what was required. The credential alone, I knew, would not have the effect that they assumed it would.

I changed the subject, and began to describe my plans to leave Nepal in a few days. What set us apart was the reality that I was an interloper into these affairs because I was in possession of a passport, which documented the fact that I did not belong. In the end, I was forced to leave Nechung and Phulmaya with their problems. I had a flight to catch and my own world to return to.

Back in Canada I began to teach a third-year course on the sociology of the family in an effort to align my teaching with my research interests. At the outset of the course, students are given an archaic anthropological definition of the family culled from one of my undergraduate courses; they are asked to critique it and then to craft their own definition of the family. The initial definition comes from a social anthropology text first published in 1963, though it was given, without irony, to the class I was attending almost thirty years later. The definition emphasized that families are based on a marriage contracted between a man and a woman who lived in a common residence, in which they shared reciprocal obligations. So much has changed since 1963. Legally obtained divorce, for example, was rare in much of the world, as were blended families; non-heteronormative families were unheard of. And the qualification that families must share a residence, which dates back to Malinowski, does not take into account the increasing number of transnational families that live in multiple residences in two, and even more, countries. My students are quick to point out these shortcomings because they live in world in which family diversity has grown within the space of a single lifetime. But they find defining what a family is to be more difficult, mainly because the family has become a "shell institution," in the words of Anthony Giddens (2003), meaning that the outward forms of the institution remain even though its primary social functions such as social reproduction and affective unity are being eroded. Simply put, the kinds of things that they are taught the family used to do their own families no longer do. Many students cling to sentimental and affective definitions of family, but it quickly becomes clear that not all of their peers share the same understanding. For every student with a sentimental, normative family there is another who is from a divorced or dysfunctional family with which they have strained relations.

A common response by many of them, year after year, is that their roommates, friends, or even rugby team members are "like family." It is among their friends that they find support, solidarity, and mutual identification. Their own biological or adoptive families live further away, and they are in the heady years of youth, discovering their own identity and becoming more autonomous. Though this response is sometimes only a way of dismissing the need to define family – students like definitions, but they don't like deconstructing and reconstructing them – it is also an acknowledgment that the family as an institution can no longer completely provide for their material and affective needs in an increasingly individualized and hyper-mobile world.

But friends are not like family. Roommates, friends, and rugby team companions make claims on us that are far weaker than those of family members, even relatives with whom we are antagonistic. Friends move on as they change addresses, occupations, and affiliations with sports teams. The fruit of friendship can be renewed only by voluntary efforts to cultivate it, and too often the conditions for growth are not favourable. Family has a way of persisting in people's lives, even when the obligations it imposes are vigorously resisted. The cultivation of family ties is an important facet of culture, and ideologies that structure it are embedded in its foundational myths and texts.

Anthropologists have long been fascinated by kinship, but what of friendship? The psychologist may claim that it is through a child's attachment to a parent that an individual first encounters and mediates an encounter with an Other, but it is through friendship that people first encounter the social Others, those for whom relations are not prescribed by kinship ideology. The myriad factors that predispose people to a friendship – class, caste, education, language, and temperament, to name a few – make possible numerous social permutations that are inherently unstable, contradictory, and sometimes unlikely. Yet they persist because they satisfy a primordial need for association. The material need for cooperation between social Others has its affective counterpart. It is good to have friends, good to be friends.

It is that good that my students are hoping to invoke through their definitions of family, but I usually protest to them that the goods of friendship are perishable. They are young and have yet to experience many of the rapid changes of adulthood. Friendships will come and go, some will last a lifetime and evolve continually; others will sour, strain, or simply become neglected. It is Nechung Lama that I am thinking of when I make these arguments to them. The many years of letters, phone calls, emails, and bank-to-bank wire transfers had come to replace our meetings in Boudhanath over salt tea and cheroots, when I was a naïve *bidhesi* conducting ethnographic research and he was an expert cultural exemplar who welcomed me and invited me to cultivate a friendship. Over those years I have watched him suffer, and I suffered too.

One night the phone rings, interrupting efforts to get my daughter to sleep. I take the receiver to the basement in order to stifle the sound. "Hello," I growl, expecting yet another offer to clean my vents, attend a seminar on a condominium sale, or send much needed assistance to children in the war-torn Middle East. A long pause, then I hear Phulmaya's voice speaking in tentative English. Talking by telephone from Nepal has become much cheaper than in the past, mere rupees per minute, thanks to wireless technology and deregulated markets that ended the monopoly of the government telephone system. Conversations between us were extremely limited in the past, but I could now speak without worrying about leaving them with a hefty telephone bill.

She begins by asking after my wife and family, then tells me that she is getting married, that she is in Kathmandu only for the wedding, and that she is marrying a Nepali man who was studying at a college in India. She is giddy with happiness. Phulmaya's dream of finding work in a thulo desh has been eclipsed by another far more realistic dream. She can leave behind the struggle that her family life had become with the collapse of Nechung's factory and the death of her mother. She can start again.

A year earlier Nechung had married a woman whom I had never met. I received this announcement in a ghostwritten letter that suggested more calculation than passion. After his wedding, Nechung had moved his home and factory from Boudhanath to another town in the Kathmandu Valley, recoiling from debt and memory. He, too, wanted to start again, though, as he had arrived in Kathmandu many years ago to weave carpets and had done little else since, working as a carpet maker was not something he could easily leave behind.

I tell Phulmaya that I am happy that she is now married and ask for her address in India so that I can send her a wedding gift. However, she forgets to tell me and says that her father, Nechung, wants to speak with me. *"Tom-ji. Sanchaai?"* I shift to Nepali, which is difficult as I have not spoken the language in a couple of years. I had been transcribing and translating the interviews I had conducted with Phulmaya a few years earlier, but with the advantage of a transcription machine I could stop, rewind, and slow the tape so that every syllable was coherent. Now Nechung was speaking at a furious clip in his thickly accented Nepali and I struggled to follow. I give him my news – we have a new house and a new baby – but I am conscious that things are not so well with him. Business is bad, he tells me, and his daughter is leaving him to live with her husband in India. I sense his sorrow.

I ask about Uttar Bhanjyang, about Helambu. "Everyone is here now," he says, "My son has also come back from India." Perhaps he did not understand, so I try again. "How is your village?" I ask. "I have not been to the village," he replies. It occurs to me that Nechung rarely referred to Uttar Bhanjyang by name, that he always used the generic *ga* when he spoke of it. There was a long pause, and I then ask if the Maoists are active there. "A little," he says, but then he goes on to say that Sonam Lama, who had been elected the leader of the Village Development Committee in 1998, was now living in Boudhanath and was working as a *thangka* painter. I did not have to ask why. We concluded our conversation and began a two-year period during which I had little contact with either Nechung or Phulmaya. As the news from Nepal darkened with insurgent and state violence, I was left to worry about the unknown consequences this might have had for my fictional kin.

Chapter Eight

Narayanhiti

In March 2009 a letter arrived from Nechung. I had not heard from him in over two years and had been quite worried that we had lost track of each other. Nepal had been torn asunder during most of that time by political and economic upheaval, and I was concerned that he had moved once again, to a new factory, back to Uttar Banjyang, or even to India to escape the chaos; or, perhaps, that our friendship had withered away unnourished, as many friendships do. Either way, I feared that I had lost him, so I was relieved to receive his letter. It was characteristically brief, written in quaint, ghostwritten English by one of the many scribes that he had employed over the years to stay in touch with me. The news in this letter was good: he tells me that he has had some personal problems, that his new factory is struggling, but also that Phulmaya and his sons are with him now. He has come home to Boudhanath. The letter seemed contented and not weighed down with the misfortune and tragedy that had filled earlier correspondences.

Nechung offers an apology for not staying in touch, then gives two cell numbers so that I could call should I ever return. His letter concludes, "How is your time going now? Nepal is a very peaceful country nowadays … I hope that you will come to Nepal as soon as possible." I immediately plan to write that it is I who should be apologizing, that I could have made more of an effort to stay in touch. Regret is what is left of friendship after it has been neglected or faded by time and distance.

Nechung was right. Nepal was more peaceful, at least relative to a few years before. Throughout the years of the insurgency I watched events from a distance, haunted by the intuition that something had to give, and that it would do so violently. In 2006 it became clear that it was the monarchy, and the royal regime whose palaces and temples defined the Kathmandu Valley, that would fall; mercifully this occurrence was not marked by the violence I had anticipated. After 2006 the king was gone, and the Maoists had locked up their weapons, at least temporarily, to join in the predictable bickering that was and is politics in Nepal. The crisis seemed to be averted, or at least fractured into a number of smaller crises that could be better managed or, preferably, ignored.

In 1987 the British Marxist scholar David Seddon (1987), in one of the first academic books I read about Nepal, predicted that declining agricultural production and dependence on food imports would lead to a crisis in Nepal that would have wide-reaching social and political consequences. According to him, Nepal's crises are rooted in the fundamentally unequal distribution of power sanctioned by the ideological structures of the Nepalese state, which was dominated by the royal regime and the feudal elites that surrounded it. This inequality was what underlay the present crisis. It was a prescient analysis, one partly shared by the Maoist politburo along with numerous others who agitated for an end to the monarchy and the hierarchical order it represented (see Seddon and Hussein 2002). Crises, in the Marxist imagination, leads to revolution by laying bare class antagonisms that come into sharp relief in times of scarcity.

But crises have always defined Nepal as a state. The Nepal we know today is the relic of the state that Prithivi Narayan Shah from the Gorkha invasions of the Kathmandu Valley created and then extended by force over a wide swathe of the Himalayas. Nepal's history drifts from one bloody crisis to another: from Prithivi Narayan Shah's mutilation of the conquered during the siege of Kirtipur in 1765, through the Kot massacre of 1847 that installed Jung Bahadur Rana as the patriarch of a hereditary dictatorship, to the brutal suppression of the Praja Parishad rebellion a century later that crushed political liberalization. Most recently, Prithivi Narayan's descendant Birendra was assassinated by his own son and the Maoist insurgency that burned through places like Rolpa, Kalikot, and Dang. Like most of our modern world, Nepal's assumed solidarities, narratives of national origin, and promises of higher purpose are fragile fictions born in violence and inhumanity. These crises would now continue, often made worse by those who fought for their resolution. Without crises, Nepal would not exist as a state.

Despite Seddon's predictions of crises and collapse and the combined efforts of the parliamentary parties and the CPN (M) to break the country through civil war, Nepal has emerged intact. If it is not stronger and more stable now, then at least it has not slipped further into an abyss. In a recent interview (*Nepali Times* 2012) Seddon issued a remarkable mea culpa by admitting that many of his darker predictions have failed to materialize. This was, in my experience, a rare occasion in which a scholar revisits and revaluates his earlier work, but that work is remarkable too because of the courage with which he made the predictions in the first place. His analysis of Nepal's antagonistic class system was probably a sounder basis for these predictions than were other ethnographic accounts of local village cultures, jat identity, and, increasingly, the corrosive effect of globalization on them, yet his predictions were partial, flawed, and too bound, perhaps, to paradigmatic bias. To be fair, and coming from a scholar who perhaps lacks the courage to develop implication into prediction, this is likely because there is so much that we cannot anticipate as events flow around us. The development of implication and power of prediction are ways in which we attempt to control that flow and to understand the current that carries us forward.

There is quite a distance from the courtyards of power to the lived reality of people like Nechung, Paljor, Nyima, and Sonam Lama. The Nepal of Prithivi Narayan Shah, Jang Bahadur Rana, BP Koirala, and even Comrade Prachanda seems an abstract reality for the people I have been writing about, except in so far as elite struggles to define, transform, or take over the state have directly impacted them. The sort of everyday crises of Nechung, Phulmaya, and my other friends are often bound too tightly to those elite struggles in our imagination. Loosening their specificity may mean that we have to set aside efforts to develop predictive implication and recognize ourselves and our friends being swept up in events that we can only partially anticipate. These idiosyncratic crises, Pierre Bourdieu's *petite misère* (1999), are sometimes, often, or perhaps too often experiences that we shape and share with them.

By the time I could bear leaving my new family life for a short time and was relieved of having to organize any more rambling faculty meetings, ten years had passed. A sabbatical in 2013 allowed me an opportunity to return to Nepal, subject to adequate funding and ethics clearance, so I was happy to announce to Nechung that I was coming back. I had resolved to shift my focus from Boudhanath and labour markets to Kirtipur and political engagement, feeling a need to break into to new territory, but I was also hoping to see my first fieldwork friends again. Speaking to Nechung on his cell phone in the autumn I told him of my plans to be there in the following spring. His phone was the only reliable way we had to stay in touch, as he had been very much on the move in the past decade. Each time I spoke to him he was in a different place – Kathmandu, Kirtipur, Helambu, Pokhara – and each time I managed to glean only a fragmentary idea about what was going on in his life. He seemed to be on the run, fleeing his misfortunes. Phulmaya was gone as well. I did gather that her marriage had failed, and that she was working as a nanny somewhere in Malaysia. Nechung was now working as carpenter.

My other friends spoke to me in a Nepali that they delivered in a measured, clearly enunciated cadence, but Nechung made little allowance for my limited competence with the language when we spoke. A telephone conversation with him was like a pop quiz as he fired his words at me in a rapid, almost interrogating fashion, his thick Helambu accent and idiom masking words I should have readily understood. I told him when I was arriving, where I was staying, and what I was planning to do, but I could not be sure that he understood. After my spring arrival I had to attempt several of the cell numbers I had, but was finally relieved to find him in Pokhara: "Tom-ji," he announced. "Where are you?" I told him that I was staying at a lodge in Sanepa. "Can you come to Pokhara?" I regretted that I could not, as I was to do work at Tribhuvan University and had only a month to do it. As best I could, I tried to explain the new work that I was doing. Nechung made no comment. "I will come to Sanepa in two days," he announced. We arranged to meet at Sanepa Chowk.

On the appointed day Nechung waved to me through the crowd, and we moved to embrace. The years had turned his once jet black hair to white. His face, though, was the same, and the contrast between them revealed the absurdity of age. I invited him up to my flat, purchasing two lukewarm bottles of orange soda on the way, a nostalgic choice, as this is what he would often serve me during my time in Boudhanath. For a couple of hours we sat and reviewed everything that had happened in the intervening years, comparing experiences. It became clear that for Nechung what had been "written in his head" wasn't anything to be wished for.

He told me that his carpet business in Boudhanath eventually had failed, because of rising piece rates for weavers and fewer weaving subcontracts from exporters. For a time he and Narendra Poudel, another friend with whom I had worked during much of my fieldwork, had collaborated on another factory in Kirtipur, but that too had failed. I was surprised that the two would attempt to work together at all; a few years previously a friend in Canada had wanted to purchase two custom-designed carpets from my friends in Kathmandu, and I ended up giving one design to Nechung and one to Narendra to weave. Both had separate carpet factories at that point. Both carpets were intended for the same room and used the same colours, but Narendra refused to cooperate with Nechung and insisted on using a different, though proximal, colour for the field of the carpet his weavers were to create. It occurred to me then that both may have been competing for my attention and for any benefits that might flow from it. I asked about Narendra, but Nechung told me that he had lost contact, and that he had not spoken to him since Kirtipur.

We then talked about his marriage, and there was some consolatory banter about men's lives with women, which would be impolitic to repeat here. We also spoke about Phulmaya who was currently in Malaysia but, he hoped, was soon to return. His elder son was back from his monastic studies in India and was living in Boudhanath. Nechung proudly told me that his son was working with an NGO, having learned to speak English well in India. I asked him about some of our friends from Helambu, and he said he did not know. He had not been back to Uttar Bhanjyang in several years.

I of course spoke of my own life since our last meeting, but felt embarrassed by the widening gap between our fortunes. Nechung had lost a wife, a son, his business, all of his worldly goods; I had lost a research grant or two and had had a couple of papers rejected by journal editors. I told him about my family, alive and intact, and I showed him pictures, but they weighed upon the conversation and we fell silent.

Nechung finally broke the silence; "I have a *karyakraam* (program) for us today. I would like to go to visit Narayanhiti, the royal palace," he said. "I have not been there until now." It was a splendid idea: the two of us, tourists together.

The towering red-brick and concrete palace tower of Narayanhiti rises at the head of Durbar Marg, one of the most modern streets in Kathmandu, lined with four-star hotels, restaurants, and expensive curio shops. The position reflects its past as the cultural and political centre of Nepal, home to a sovereign believed to be a living god. It is still surrounded by high fences and concertina wire, though the wooden observation posts that once bristled with heavily armed soldiers are now empty. The regime that it accommodated has now been swept aside in another crisis, but where the palaces of earlier sovereigns were demolished and replaced by those of their successors, Narayanhiti suffers a more inglorious fate. It has become a museum, an anachronism that even more permanently renders powerless the authority of a divine sovereign. In what was the guardhouse that once protected the main gate from the multitudes that marched up Durbar Marg to confront this power, a few blue-shirted policemen rock back and forth on wooden chairs, twirling their lathis as visitors are ushered through the metal detector at the gate before entering the palace grounds. Entry tickets are sold: 100 rupees for Nepalese visitors, 300 rupees for other South Asians, and 500 rupees for all others.

Narayanhiti, the museum, is haunted by the memories of the 2001 assassination of King Birendra by his own son, intoxicated with privilege and armed with patricidal rage. But there are other ghosts as well, for the palace Narayanhiti, meaning the spring of Narayan, avatar of the Hindu god Vishnu, has long been associated with the fraternal violence of Nepal's ruling elites. In 1885 Jang Bahadur Rana's brother, Ranodip Singh, was assassinated at Narayanhiti by his own nephews in a palace later destroyed by his successor Bir Shamsher, perhaps to obliterate any memory of the murder and his own complicity in it. In its place, Bir built a massive Rana-style palace that became the residence of Nepal's kings, who held little power during the Rana regime. That palace was levelled, in turn, in the early reign of Mahendra, the assassinated king's father, who asserted the dominance of his monarchy after the decline of the Ranas. Each transition from one regime to another entailed the destruction of a palace beside Narayan's waters.

Mahendra's Narayanhiti was completed in 1969, based on a design by the American architect Benjamin Polk. Polk's Narayanhiti, built to Mahendra's specifications, fused modernist and traditional Nepalese forms in a way that differentiates it from the architectural legacy of the Ranas that still figure prominently in the Kathmandu cityscape. The Keshar Mahal, which houses the Department of Education located nearby, is an example of Rana opulence that emulates British colonial form while eschewing the architectural legacy of Prithivi Narayan Shah and his successors. The contemporary Narayanhiti's prominent pagoda-style tower, which dominates Durbar Marg, evokes the pre-Rana style as a reassertion of that succession. The exterior of the new palace is unremarkable red-brick with little exterior elaboration. Other than the portico and a concrete tower that soars beside it, there is little to distinguish this building from the Tribhuvan airport terminal, which was built at the same time. As palaces go, it is a fairly austere place, a reflection of Mahendra's aversion to ostentatious taste (Ranjit 2009).

Nechung remembers coming here as a boy with his father, when the oppressive gates were opened to people being offered a *tikka* blessing by the king for the Dasain festival. This was the only time that the sovereign touched, literally, the lives of his subjects, his divinity mediated by vermilion yogurt and rice that marked his subjects' foreheads. It was also the only time a commoner could enter these gates and glimpse the regal opulence inside. As we pass through the metal detectors and I raise my arms for an additional sweep with a hand-held detector, I think of the king, now dead twelve years, by his formal title. I remember Shree Paanch Birendra Bir Bikram Shah as he appeared in most photographs of the time, wearing severe aviation sunglasses like a Bollywood villain or Augusto Pinochet. Monarchy to me is a relic, a shadow of relevance, which in its constitutional form is colourful, harmless, and largely insignificant, but Nechung speaks of this memory with fondness and reverence. We are in the same space, we are experiencing different places.

Nechung was no monarchist. He was opposed to Pashupati Shamsher Rana's representative in Uttar Banjyang, though his opposition might be more for personal than for ideological reasons. Nechung appeared to be uninterested in politics, for like many Nepalese he followed prevailing political tendencies and was largely preoccupied with his own work and family. But here at the gate he appears nostalgic for his king, though perhaps the sentiment is less for the person than for the certainly and stability that the past affords. It is through this conflicted nostalgia that he is experiencing Narayanhiti; it touches him in ways that it cannot possibly touch me.

Early May is the hottest and driest month in Kathmandu, and the royal ground shows signs of drought as much as any other green space in the city. The clay flowerpots that line the grand staircase that leads into the main hall are filled with baked, cracked earth. A massive wood archway, carved in Newari style, announces the entrance to the palace. The two front doors, each bearing swastikas, symbols of good fortune, swing inwards to the Kaski Baithak, the main reception hall. We are temporarily blinded, coming in from the bright sun, but as our eyes adjust, we see that the king's outward restraint is not evident inside. Nechung gasps as the light reveals the grand hall with its towering, chandeliered ceiling. It is cool inside, but still dim and, to me if not to

Nechung, the Kaski Baithak appears faded and unused. A guard warns us not to sit in the chairs that line the walls. Large oil portraits of Shah ancestors stare down at us wearing their feathered headdresses and weighed down with chests of medals and honours.

Our tour takes us to the west wing of the palace, which was designed to entertain – and perhaps confine – foreign dignitaries. The crowd stops before a wide lounge lit by the afternoon sun flooding through high windows. The guard returns to her post and I wait for a guide to narrate the scene, but no one speaks. We have been left alone to interpret what we are seeing. I remember a pamphlet we collected at the door that Nechung cannot read, as it is in English only. I tell him as best I can that this room was reserved for the leisure of foreign guests, whose access to the royal family must have been carefully restricted. The furniture looks old and uncomfortable; an antique box television sits in one corner with what looks like a remote control as big as a shoe box sitting on top. I notice that the ashtrays in the room are attached to stuffed animal legs which I try to identify. "Are these buffalo?" I ask. "No, elephant " answers another guest from across the room. He smiles. He is tall and well dressed and introduces himself as being from Jhapa, a province in the far east. Over his head a gharial skin has been stretched and nailed into place.

Our group moves along compelled only by what is to be seen next, and we enter another room lined with brass religious statuary. Nechung gasps again and pauses to reflect on a large, ornate, wooden model of the Pashupatinath temple while I escape the crowd by moving on ahead into a narrow hallway. The walls are lined with photographs of dignitaries who have visited this wing over the years; Queen Elizabeth and Prince Philip, Henry Kissinger, Marshal Tito, Kurt Waldheim. Tuxedos and tiaras. Nechung joins me, but pays no attention to the photos, as they are only faces to him. I read in the pamphlet that the large bedroom off to the side once accommodated Queen Elizabeth on a state visit. The room is far from stately, the bed square and severe, the curtains thick, conventional. I try, but fail, to imagine the queen as a guest here, but then an uninvited image of Tito reclining on the bed arises, so I flee the room.

Nechung and I continue along hallways that open up into well-appointed rooms – rooms, the pamphlet tells us, for dignitaries to rest before eating, rooms for eating, rooms for resting after eating. Each room is named after one of Nepal's many regions and is labelled at the entrance in both roman and Devanagiri script. I note than many of the regions are those that until recently had been the epicentre of the Maoist revolt in the west. "This is Rolpa!" exclaims one man in our group. He peers inside the room: antique sofas, drab Aubusson carpets, more stools crafted from dead wildlife. He looks disappointed as we move on.

"Where is Tanahun?" asks once member of our group of no one in particular. "Where is Morang?" asks another. Nechung looks at me, "Let's look for Sindhupalchok." So much prestige rides on which district is designated to which room. We emerge into the rear of the enormous Kaski Baithak and ascend the grand staircase to the throne room, appropriately named Gorkha Baithak, after Prithivi Narayan Shah's home district, which occupies the interior of the pagoda tower seen from the street. It is clearly a room intended to impress. The king's golden throne sits at the centre of the eastern wall, directly under an enormous chandelier that hangs from a sixty-foot-high ceiling that rises in the style of the shikhara temples found throughout the Kathmandu Valley. Four enormous serpentine struts rise from each corner of the room to meet at the apex of the ceiling, where gaudily painted scenes depict powerful Hindu figures that are intended as metaphors of royal power. To my eyes, the paintings are unremarkable and lend the room the air of an amusement park, but Nechung appears awed. At the very pinnacle of the room, higher than the throne, the chandelier, and the technicolor goddesses, an air conditioner on the ceiling whirs noisily.

We are conducted by guards through the doors beside the throne. As we pass, I note that some guests have tossed rupee notes and paise on the throne, perhaps for supplication or for a wish to come true. No one in our group offers anything.

The room directly behind the throne is identified as Mahendra's private study, and it appears to be as it was in 1970, with rotary phones, an old dictation machine, and high shelves of books in both Nepali and English. I wonder why the long-dead Mahendra's office is preserved in all this opulent irrelevance. Directly behind is Birendra's study and smoking room, where many of the books on the shelves are colourful picture books or guides that could be found on the bookshelves of shops down the road in Thamel. Were these books what he was reading before his death, or were they placed there by curators seeking to embellish Narayanhiti's past for present purposes? There is no computer, no advanced communication technology at all, and I doubt, even there, whether the museum has been restored to what might have been in 2001 or earlier.

There appears to be no reference anywhere to the last royal inhabitant of the palace, Birendra's brother Gyanendra: it is as if he had never occupied the palace at all. Later, as the tour is being directed out to the gardens, I notice a plain chair sitting incongruously at the rear of the Kaski Baithak. Taped to the back is a sheet of white A5 paper that informs us, in English, that this is the chair that Gyanendra sat on when he announced his abdication on television in 2006. It seemed an afterthought amid the gloomy splendour of Narayanhiti, an ignominious end to a dynasty.

We emerge from the palace and follow the arrows designating the tour route to the western side of the main palace building. There are numerous other structures here: military barracks and the western gate that opens onto the Kantipath opposite the Keshar Mahal. From the northeast corner of the palace the vast gardens spread, and the arrows lead to a sign posted at what looks to be foundations of some building nestled in long, yellow grass. They are what is left of the Tribhuvan Sadan, the small building in which Dipendra's patricidal rage was played out. The sign informs us that the Queen Mother Ratna, Mahendra's widow and mother to the assassinated king, ordered that the building be demolished following these events – a decision that helped fuel a widespread belief even today that there were unseen forces behind Birendra's assassination (Whelpton 2005).

Behind us in a rhododendron garden a sign in Devanagiri script draws our attention to bullet holes in the north wall of the palace. Some of them penetrate deep into the red brick; some Nepalese boys explore the holes with their fingers, as if to reassure themselves that they are real. They chatter rapidly about the various conspiracy theories that reject the official version of events; I can hear only names: Gyanendra, Paras (his playboy son who is deeply unpopular with the people), Grijia Koirala (the then prime minister), the Maoists.

As they continue to debate heatedly among themselves, I turn to Nechung and ask what he thinks. "I don't know," he shrugs as we drift away from the others. Nechung is quiet now. We cross a small bridge arched over a shallow stream that runs from what was the ornate central fountain to the swimming pool. It was here that Dipendra is said to have shot himself, just after dispatching his mother and brother Nirajan nearby. The fountain plume, reputed to be in the shape of peacock tail, is turned off now, the swimming pool is empty. In a fenced-off area ahead of us a child's swing set sits abandoned in the tall grass.

Figure 8.1. Tourists outside the gates of the Narayanhiti Museum, May 2013.

Nechung and I follow the walkway through the garden, past the bandshell and out to the exit. "He was a very rich man," he says after a time. "He was very greedy." We stop to retrieve my camera and backpack from the guard house – photography is not permitted inside – a prohibition, I figured, that indicated that Narayanhiti was still held to be a sacred place to some. We pose for few pictures and then step out into the heated bustle of Durbar Marg. Nechung and I walk without speaking, he seeming absorbed in his own thoughts. We pass through Thamel, rubbing shoulders with tourists and dodging mountaineering equipment hung onto the streets on display, then enter the narrow alleys of the inner city. Finally we come to New Road, pressed with people and traffic, and Nechung pauses for a cigarette. He offers me one; even though I no longer smoke, in the past we shared cigarettes in day-to-day reciprocity, so I accept. The smoke tempts, and my head begins a familiar spin. Nechung asks, "Can you come to Pokhara?" I say that I have a busy schedule in Kirtipur, and that I cannot get away, as I must leave in three weeks' time. "Then we can meet in Boudhanath tomorrow?" he asks. I reply, "Not tomorrow, I have a meeting in Kirtipur. Can we meet there the day after?"

We flag down a taxi and Nechung begins negotiating the fare to my hotel. The driver will not budge from his price, however, arguing that he needs to turn around and backtrack, owing to the one-way traffic on the New Road. Nechung looks irritated as I take his hand in mine and promise to meet him in two days. There is an edge to his voice, and I am not sure if it was meant for the taxi driver or for me. The tour of Narayanhiti seems to have plunged him into an introspective mood; the palace had revealed to him something that he did not want to know.

Clifford Geertz, in the essay "Thinking as a Moral Act: Ethical Dimensions of Anthropological Fieldwork in New States," wrote that the idea that the fieldworker and the informant are members of the same moral community "is never really completely convincing for any of the participants" because we are constantly confronted by the globally structured inequalities that enable and/or constrain our life chances (1968, 154). To say that we are members of the same community ignores the moral and ethical tensions that arise from that disparity and implies a deceit – though more a form of self-deception than an intentional ethnographic tactic. Perhaps *conceit* is a better word, the vainglorious insinuation of the ethnographer into the lives of Others. The idea that we share a moral community with our fieldwork friends begs the question of whose morality.

Nechung and I were members of a moral community that held, despite the centrifugal forces of class, race, caste, and privilege, but it was a moral community only in so far as both of us were conducting ourselves with each other in action. Mutual engagement in social action does not mean that the motivation behind that action is shared, nor does it mean that the consequences of that action will be equally distributed. Those things are determined outside the community, and each participant has only an incomplete and contingent understanding of how those forces can be bargained with.

The various moral acts that established our community were probably not rooted in the same conceptual ground. The acts of gift giving, of appealing for and offering assistance, and of sharing information were components of our friendship, and this relationship would not have been possible without them, But they alone conjure only the cultural logic of social reciprocity, the Maussian calculation of social cohesion and social ends. But it is worth recalling that what John Dewey (1960) described as customary morality – that is, moral conduct prescribed by cultural authority – is often complemented by reflective morality, the ability of moral actors to weigh alternative courses of action in pursuit of a desired good. The pursuit of desired ends, Dewey warned us, cannot be banished from morality. Too often our ethnographic accounts proceed as though actions are performances of customary morality, cultural texts, or authorities, ignoring their reflective character. Nevertheless, I cannot help but conclude that a powerful customary logic was in operation on Nechung's part, a logic evoked by his description of me as aaphno maanchhe and his deft deployment of gifts and hospitality as an overture to friendship.

On the other hand, incontrovertible reflective morality in research seems expected of fieldworking ethnographers, even though much of what we do is prescribed by scholarly, disciplinary, or institutional standards that are customary motivations for our action – not the cultural logic of gift giving, but that of grant writing, scientific discourse, and peer review. My participation in this moral community was motivated, as Nechung's was, by material desire. He hoped that our friendship would lead to his greater prosperity and prestige, while I hoped for assistance and data. But that is not all that I desired. I wanted companionship and saw in Nechung qualities that attracted me, not the least of which was his ambition to become successful, to become an important and modern man.

In the end, I became a participant observer in his failure, or rather in the tragedies that have marked his life after we came to know each other through my fieldwork. His collapse as a carpet entrepreneur has been experienced by many other small-scale producers, and even some of the larger ones, as the market for Tibeto-Nepalese carpets has declined since 1995. The deaths of his wife, his son, and the prolonged absences of his other children hastened his decline even further. Some may believe that there is a moral imperative for friends to come to each other's aid in such a time, but such assistance cannot ensure a better outcome. Friends can often do more, but they do not because of how they weigh the consequences of their actions in the flux of events that are ambiguous, contingent, and entangled. At any point in the last decade I could have let our friendship lapse, but I did not, and that in itself is a moral act.

In the essay noted above, Geertz also provocatively comments that "many anthropologists leave the field seeing tears in the eyes of their informants that, I feel quite sure, are not really there" (1968, 151).

I am not sure that Nechung shed any tears for me as we parted at Narayanhiti that day; the sadness he felt may have been because the tragedies evoked by the palace's gloomy interiors reminded him of his own losses. It may have also reminded him that the hopes he had invested in our friendship had not paid the dividends he had expected. Neither of us could read what was "written in our heads." For some the remedy for indeterminate moral reflections are recourse to ethical rules that are better applied in retrospect or to forms of objective scientism in which there is no room at all for tears. For me, the fact that there may be few tears on Nechung's side does not mean that there should be none on my own.

Two days after our visit to Naryanhiti, I call Nechung's cell as I set out for Boudhanath by taxi. He answers, and I tell him that I am on my way. "I am in Pokhara" he declares "I have to get back to work, because I need to work when I can." Nechung is no longer in a position to work at his own pace; he is compelled to work as demanded of him. I am disappointed that he has been called away, but he tells me that he will come back to see me in Kathmandu before I leave.

The taxi arrives and I emerge at the stupa gate. The entrance fee for foreigners is 500 rupees and I pay, reminded that I am a privileged stranger here. In the past I walked through these gates to get to our flat up the road and often met friends, shopkeepers, people that I had been working with in the carpet factories along the way. There was no fee. I take the entrance ticket, which warns me to produce it when asked by any attendant inside, and walk into the shiny new stupa square. Byrarung khashor stares indifferently to the south, held by sweeping petals of yellow paint. Fresh cobblestones border the stupa. Numerous women with bamboo brooms sweep away the dust, and even more numerous police in blue fatigues watch the crowds carefully; a few months earlier, a Tibetan dissident had immolated himself here, hoping to mingle his ashes with the dust.

In my notes I have an old landline number for Narendra Poudel. It has been more than a decade since we last spoke and I am not sure the number still works, but I try it anyway. Incredibly, he answers, and minutes later we embrace at the stupa gate. We spend the next few hours reminiscing over tea as his son, now an engineering student at one of Kathmandu's new private universities, hunches over a desktop computer browsing my Facebook page. Later I wonder at how different Nechung and Narendra's lives have been: both men were small-scale carpet producers who came to Kathmandu from Sindhupalchok; Narendra's village was located on a ridge of hills east of Uttar Bhanyang; and both lost their businesses in 2005. Narendra, however, seems to have landed on his feet because of a combination of wise investments and the support of three successful sons, one of whom is currently working in the United States. Narendra is an educated Brahmin, which I think lent him advantages that Nechung lacked as he tried to adjust to his changed circumstances.

A few days later, Nechung telephones and apologizes for not being able to be with me. He is unable to get away from work. It may be that he had been compelled to return because of a busy schedule, perhaps because the oncoming monsoon would slow construction of the project he was employed on. I don't know, but I cannot help feeling that my presence is a reminder of all that he has suffered over the previous decade.

Before I depart I leave him a small gift package at my hotel: a small bottle of Niagara ice wine and a large, framed print of the two of us together standing in front of Narayanhiti. Back in Canada now I await another phone call, another ghostwritten letter. I know that it will come. As this story draws to a close, I still hope that its final chapter is not yet written in our heads and that other more hopeful, more fruitful conclusions are still possible.

Selected Glossary of Nepali and Tibetan Terms

aaphno maanchhe Literally "our own people." It refers to informal networks of kin, fellow villagers, and associates that form a basis for social life in much of Nepal.

chöten The Tibetan name for the hemispherical Buddhist monuments found throughout Himalayan Nepal and other regions where Buddhists live throughout South and Southeast Asia; also known as *stupa*, from the Sanskrit.

dal bhaat Common daily meal for most Nepalis, consisting of rice, lentil soup (*dal*), and vegetable or meat curry.

dharma The fundamental knowledge of suffering and the liberation from suffering taught by the Buddha and by the Mahayana and Vajrayana gurus, who later elaborated on this knowledge.

duhkha Sorrow or suffering.

gonpa A Tibetan Buddhist temple, usually consisting of an indoor space with a large altar at one end containing religious objects and depictions of Buddhist deities.

Guru Rinpoche The Tibetan name for the eighth-century Tantric guru, Padmsambhava, who is a central figure in the Nyingmapa form of the Buddhism of Helambu.

guthi State allocations of land for religious purposes, such as the construction of gonpa and associated property.

janajati The various ethnic groups or "tribes" in Nepal that are not part of the traditional Hindu *varna* system of castes. They include Tibeto-Burmese groups that claim to be Nepal's "indigenous" people. In practice many of these groups have been Sanskritized and integrated into Nepal's Hindu social structure.

jan andolan Literally "people's movement," which refers to the uprisings of both 1990, which established a constitutional monarchy, and 2006, which brought the monarchy to an end.

jati Expansive term for caste that includes the castes defined under the four Hindu *varnas* (in Nepal: Brahmin, Chetris, Vaishya, and Sudra) as well as other ethnic groups, including the Magar, Tamang, Sherpa, Yolmo, Newar, and other cultural and linguistic groups that are commonly described as *janajati*.

khata Silk scarves given as a sign of respect in Tibetan Buddhist communities.

khukri Curved knife commonly found throughout Nepal, used both by the military and as a common tool for farmers and cooks.

lathi Thick bamboo sticks used by police for crowd control.

lahure Literally a person from Lahore in what is now Pakistan, but in Nepal this word traditionally referred to Gurkha soldiers recruited to the British Army (who reported to Lahore for service). Currently also used by some to describe Nepali migrants who travel abroad to work.

lakh The Nepali unit of measurement for 100,000 rupees.

lama A Tibetan religious teacher, as well as a surname for many of the Yolmo people of Helambu and for specific Tamang clans.

mani Stones inscribed with Tibetan prayers that are found throughout the Himalayas.

momo Tibetan dumpling commonly filled with meat or potatoes.

paati Small shelter to accommodate travellers or mourners near a cremation ground.

panchayat Literally "assembly of five." It refers to the five elders who traditionally formed the leadership of a village council. King Mahendra replaced multiparty democracy with his own, autocratic "panchayat democracy" in 1960. Even after the restoration of multiparty democracy in 1990, village councils were still popularly called "panchayats."

puja Buddhist or Hindu rituals of worship.

raksi Distilled liquor made from fermented millet or rice; commonly found in Nepal's hills.

rinpoche A high lama and religious teacher.

saahuji Literally "shopkeeper," but also used to identify the proprietor of a carpet-weaving factory.

stupa Nepali term for the Tibetan chöten (see the definition above).

tempo Three-wheeled mini taxis and buses that ply the streets of Kathmandu.

thekadaar Literally "contractor," but usually refers to a middleman (or woman) who collects labourers for an industry. Many carpet weavers, for example, were contracted by a thekadaar, not the factory owner.

thulo desh Literally "big country," by which is generally meant countries in the developed world, such as those in Europe or North America.

References

Adams, Vincanne. 1996. *Tigers in the Snow and Other Virtual Sherpas*. Princeton: Princeton University Press.
Appadurai, Arjun. 1998. *Modernity at Large: Cultural Dimensions of Globalization*. Minneapolis: University of Minneapolis Press.
Anderson, Benedict. 1991. *Imagined Communities: Reflections on the Origin and Spread of Nationalism*. London: Verso.
Asad, Talal. 1991. "From the History of Colonial Anthropology to the Anthropology of Western Hegemony." In *Colonial Situations: Essays on the Contextualization of Ethnographic Knowledge*, ed. George Stocking. 314–24. Madison: University of Wisconsin Press.
Bakhtin, Mikhail. 1981. *The Dialogic Imagination: Four Essays*. Edited by Michael Holquist. Austin: University of Texas Press.
Bauman, Zygmunt. 1997. *Postmodernity and its Discontents*. Cambridge: Polity Press.
Bauman, Zygmunt. 1998. *Globalization: The Human Consequences*. New York: Colombia University Press.
Behar, Ruth. 1996. *The Vulnerable Observer: Anthropology That Breaks Your Heart*. Boston: Beacon Press.
Benjamin, Walter. 1968. *Illuminations*. New York: Harcourt, Brace and World.
Bishop, Naomi. 1998. *Himalayan Herders*. New York: Harcourt Brace.
Bista, Dor Bahadur. 1991. *Fatalism and Development*. New Delhi: Orient Longman.
Blim, Michael. 2005. "The Moral Significance of Petty Capitalism." In *Petty Capitalism and Globalization: Flexibility, Entrepreneurship and Economic Development*, ed. Alan Smart and Josephine Smart. 253–70. Albany: State University of New York Press.
Bourdieu, Pierre. 1998. *Practical Reason*. Stanford: Stanford University Press.

Bourdieu, Pierre, et al. 1999. *The Weight of the World: Social Suffering in Contemporary Society*. Stanford: Stanford University Press.

Butz, David, and Kathryn Besio. 2004. "The Value of Autoethnography for Field Research in Transcultural Settings." *Professional Geographer* 56 (3): 350–60.

Campbell, Ben. 1997. "The Heavy Loads of Tamang Identity." In *Nationalism and Ethnicity in a Hindu Kingdom: The Politics of Culture in Contemporary Nepal*, ed. David Gellner, Joanna Pfaff-Czarnecka, and John Whelpton. 205–35. Amsterdam: Harwood Academic.

Clarke, Graham. 1980. "A Helambu History." *Journal of Nepal Research Centre* 4: 1–38.

Clifford, James, and George E. Marcus. 1986. *Writing Culture: The Poetics and Politics of Ethnography*. Berkeley: University of California Press.

Comaroff, John, and Jean Comaroff. 2009. *Ethnicity, Inc.* Chicago: University of Chicago Press. http://dx.doi.org/10.7208/chicago/9780226114736.001.0001.

Constable, Nicole. 1997. *Maid to Order in Hong Kong: Stories of Filipina Workers*. Ithaca: Cornell University Press.

Corsaro, William, and Luisa Molinari. 2008. "Entering and Observing Children's Worlds: A Reflection on a Longitudinal Ethnography of Early Education in Italy." In *Research with Children: Perspectives and Practices*, ed. Pia Christensen and Allison James. 239–59. New York: Routledge.

CWIN. 1992. *Misery behind the Looms: Child Labourers in the Carpet Factories of Nepal*. Kathmandu: Child Workers in Nepal Concerned Centre.

Denwood, Philip. 1974. *The Tibetan Carpet*. Warminster: Aris and Phillips.

Denzin, Norman K. 2003. "Performing [Auto] Ethnography Politically." *Review of Education, Pedagogy & Cultural Studies* 25 (3): 257–78. http://dx.doi.org/10.1080/10714410390225894.

Denzin, Norman K. 2006. "Analytic Autoethnography, or, Déjà Vu All Over Again." *Journal of Contemporary Ethnography* 35 (4): 419–28. http://dx.doi.org/10.1177/0891241606286985.

Desjarlais, Robert. 1992. *Body and Emotion: The Aesthetics of Illness and Healing in the Nepal Himalayas*. Philadelphia: University of Pennsylvania Press.

Desjarlais, Robert. 2003. *Sensory Biographies: Lives and Deaths among Nepal's Yolmo Buddhists*. Berkeley: University of California Press.

Dewey, John. 1960. *Theory of a Moral Life*. New York: Holt, Reinhart and Winston.

Ellis, Carolyn. 2004. *The Ethnographic I: A Methodological Novel about Autoethnography*. Walnut Creek, CA: Altamira Press.

Fisher, James. 1990. *Sherpas: Reflections of Change in Himalayan Nepal*. Berkeley: University of California Press.

Fisher, James 2007. "Identity in Nepal: Ethnic, Individual, Political." *Revista de Antropologia* 36 (2): 155–74.

Gamburd, Michelle. 2000. *The Kitchen Spoon's Handle: Transnationalism and Sri Lanka's Migrant Housemaids*. Ithaca: Cornell University Press.

Geertz, Clifford. 1968. "Thinking as a Moral Act: Ethical Dimensions of Anthropological Fieldwork in the New States." *Antioch Review* 28 (2): 139–58. http://dx.doi.org/10.2307/4610913.

Geertz, Clifford. 1988. *Works and Lives: the Anthropologist as Author*. Stanford: Stanford University Press.

Gibb, Camilla. 2005a. "An Anthropologist Undone." In *Autoethnographies: The Anthropology of Academic Practices*, ed. Anne Meneley and Donna J. Young. 218–28. Peterborough, ON: Broadview Press.

Gibb, Camilla. 2005b. *Sweetness in the Belly*. Toronto: Doubleday Canada.

Giddens, Anthony. 1990. *The Consequences of Modernity*. Stanford: Stanford University Press.

Giddens, Anthony. 2003. *Runaway World*. New York: Routledge.

Gombo, Ugen. 1985. "Tibetan Refugees in the Kathmandu Valley: Adaptation of a Population in Exile." PhD diss., State University of New York at Stony Brook.

Graner, Elvira. 2003. "Migration and Sustainable Development: Carpet Workers in the Kathmandu Valley." In *Translating Development: The Case of Nepal*, ed. M. Domroes. 247–67. New Delhi: Manohar Press.

Guta, Thomas. 1992. "The Weavers of Tradition." In *Nepal Traveller: The Nepalese-Tibetan Carpet*. Trade magazine, Kathmandu. January, 66–74.

Haggerty, Kevin. 2004. "Ethics Creep: Governing Social Science Research in the Name of Ethics." *Qualitative Sociology* 27 (4): 391–414. http://dx.doi.org/10.1023/B:QUAS.0000049239.15922.a3.

Harvey, David. 1989. *The Condition of Post-Modernity*. Oxford: Basil Blackwell.

Hastrup, Kirsten. 1997. "The Dynamics of Anthropological Theory." *Cultural Dynamics* 9 (3): 351–71. http://dx.doi.org/10.1177/092137409700900305.

Holmberg, David. 1989. *Order in Paradox: Myth, Ritual and Exchange among Nepal's Tamang*. Ithaca: Cornell University Press.

Heider, Karl G. 1975. "What Do People Do? Dani Auto-Ethnography." *Journal of Anthropological Research* 31: 3–17.

Hunt, Lynn. 2007. *Inventing Human Rights: A History*. New York: W.W. Norton.

Jackson, Michael. 1998. *Minima Ethnographica: Intersubjectivity and the Anthropological Project*. Chicago: University of Chicago Press.

Justice, Judith. 1986. *Policies, Plans and People: Foreign Aid and Health Development*. Berkeley: University of California Press.

Kondos, Alex. 1987. "The Question of 'Corruption' In Nepal." *Mankind* 17 (1): 15–29.

Luhmann, Niklas. 1988. "Familiarity, Confidence, Trust: Problems and Alternatives." In *Trust: Making and Breaking Cooperative Relations*, ed. Diego Gambetta. 94–107. Oxford: Basil Blackwell.

Lhalungpa, Lobsang Phuntshock. 1979. *The Life of Milarepa*, London: Granada.

Marcus, George. 1998. Review of *Auto/Ethnography: Rewriting the Self and the Social*. American Journal of Sociology 104 (2): 582–5. http://dx.doi.org/10.1086/210075.

Marx, Karl, and Friedrich Engels. 1967. *The German Ideology*. New York: International Publishers.

Misztal, Barbara A. 1996. *Trust in Modern Societies*. Cambridge: Polity Press.

Mitchell, Timothy. 2000. *Questions of Modernity*. Minneapolis: University of Minnesota Press.

Montaigne, Michel de. 1965. *The Complete Essays of Montaigne*. Edited by Donald M. Frame. Stanford: Stanford University Press.

Moran, Peter. 2004. *Buddhism Observed: Exiles and Tibetan Dharma in Kathmandu*. London, New York: Routledge. http://dx.doi.org/10.4324/9780203379448.

Nepali Times. 2012. "Interview: A Dangerous Racism." *Nepali Times* online. http://nepalitimes.com/~nepalitimes/news.php?id=19569#.VFpcDsmr_mk. Accessed 05/11/2014.

O'Neill, Tom. 2001. "Nepalese Entrepreneurial Communities and the European Hand Knotted Carpet Market." In *Plural Globalities in Multiple Localities: New World Border*, ed. Josephine Smart and Martha Rees. 149–65. Lanham, MD: University Press of America (co-published with Society for Economic Anthropology).

O'Neill, Tom. 2004 "Weaving Wages, Indebtedness and Remittances in the Nepalese Carpet Industry." *Human Organization* 63(2): 211–20.

O'Neill, Tom. 2005. "Labour Standard Regulation and the Modernization of Small-Scale Carpet Production in Kathmandu Nepal." In Smart and Smart, *Petty Capitalists and Globalization*. 201–25.

Ortner, Sherry. 1989. *High Religion: A Cultural and Political History of Sherpa Buddhism*. Princeton: Princeton University Press.

Ortner, Sherry. 2001. *Life and Death on Mt. Everest: Sherpa and Himalayan Mountaineering*. Princeton: Princeton University Press.

Parreñas, Rhacel Salazar. 2001. *Servants of Globalization: Women, Migration and Domestic Work*. Stanford: Stanford University Press.

Pelias, Ronald J. 2004. *A Methodology of the Heart: Evoking Academic and Daily Life*. Lanham, MD: Altamira Press.

Pigg, Stacey. 1992. "Inventing Social Categories through Place: Social Representations and Development in Nepal." *Comparative Studies in Society and History* 34 (3): 491–513. http://dx.doi.org/10.1017/S0010417500017928.

Pratt, Mary Louise. 1986. "Fieldwork in Common Places." In *Writing Culture: The Poetics and Politics of Ethnography*, ed. James Clifford and George E. Marcus. 27–50. Berkeley: University of California Press.

Pratt, Mary Louise.1992. *Imperial Eyes: Travel Writing and Transculturation*. London: Routledge. http://dx.doi.org/10.4324/9780203163672.

Qvortrup, Jens. 2008. "Macroanalysis of Childhood." In *Research with Children: Perspectives and Practices*, ed. Pia Christensen and Allison James. 66–87. New York: Routledge.

Raeper, William, and Martin Hoftun. 1992. *Spring Awakening: An Account of the 1990 Revolution in Nepal*. New Delhi, New York: Viking Press.

Ranjit, Sushmita. 2009. "A Thought over Narayanhiti Palace." *Spaces: Art, Architecture, Interior*. http://www.spacesnepal.com. Accessed 11/05/2014.

Reed-Danahay, Deborah, ed. 1997. *Auto/Ethnography: Rewriting the Self and the Social*. New York: Berg.

Regmi, Mahesh C. 1988. *An Economic History of Nepal, 1846–1901*. Varanasi: Nath Publishing House.

Rorty, Richard. 1989. *Contingency, Irony, and Solidarity*. Cambridge: Cambridge University Press. http://dx.doi.org/10.1017/CBO9780511804397.

Seddon, David. 1987. *Nepal: A State of Poverty*. New Delhi: Vikas Publishing House.

Seddon, David, and Karim Hussein. 2002. "The Consequences of Conflict: Livelihoods and Development in Nepal." Livelihoods and Chronic Conflict Working Paper Series. London: Overseas Development Institute.

Seddon, David, Jaganath Adhikari, and Ganesh Gurung. 2001. *The New Lahures: Foreign Employment and Remittance Economy of Nepal*. Kathmandu: Nepal Institute of Development Studies.

Seddon, David, Jaganath Adhikari, and Ganesh Gurung. 2002. "Foreign Labour Migration and the Remittance Economy of Nepal." *Critical Asian Studies* 34 (1): 19–40. http://dx.doi.org/10.1080/146727102760166581.

Shah, Nasra M., and Indu Menon. 1999. "Chain Migration through the Social Networks: Experience of Labour Migrants in Kuwait." International *Migration (Geneva, Switzerland)* 37 (2): 361–82. http://dx.doi.org/10.1111/1468-2435.00076.

Sharma, Prayag Raj. 1992. "How to Tend This Garden." *Himal* (June).

Shrestha, Nanda R. 2008. "'Misery Is My Company Now': Nepal's Peasantry in the Face of Failed Development." *Journal of Peasant Studies* 35 (3): 452–75. http://dx.doi.org/10.1080/03066150802340438.

Smart, Alan, and Josephine Smart, eds. 2005. *Petty Capitalism and Globalization: Flexibility, Entrepreneurship and Economic Development*. Albany: State University of New York Press.

Stark, Oded. 1995. *Altruism and Beyond: An Economic Analysis of Transfers and Exchanges within Families and Groups*. Cambridge: Cambridge University Press. http://dx.doi.org/10.1017/CBO9780511493607.

Stoller, Paul. 2004. *Stranger in the Village of the Sick: A Memoir of Cancer, Sorcery, and Healing*. Boston: Beacon Press.

Stoller. 2007. "Ethnography/Memoir/Imagination/Story." *Anthropology and Humanism* 32 (2): 178–91. http://dx.doi.org/10.1525/ahu.2007.32.2.178.

Tedlock, Dennis. 1983. *The Spoken Word and the Work of Interpretation*. Philadelphia: University of Pennsylvania Press. http://dx.doi.org/10.9783/9780812205305.

Tocqueville, Alexis de. 1990. *Democracy in America*. New York: Vintage Books.

Whelpton, John. 1997. "Political Identity in Nepal: State, Nation and Community." In *Nationalism and Ethnicity in a Hindu Kingdom: The Politics of Culture in Contemporary Nepal*, ed. David Gellner, Joanna Pfaff-Czarnecka, and John Whelpton. 39–78. Amsterdam: Harwood Academic.

Whelpton, John. 2005. *A History of Nepal*. Cambridge: Cambridge University Press.

Zivetz, Laura. 1992. *Private Enterprise and the State in Modern Nepal*. Oxford: Oxford University Press.

Index

aaphno maanchhe, 70–1, 75–6, 8, 83, 117, 151, 155
Anderson, Benedict, 49
anthropology, 9, 10–11, 12–17, 23, 45
Appadurai, Arjun, 24
Asad, Talal, 23
autoethnography, 11–14, 17–18

Bakhtin, Mikhail, 17
Bauman, Zygmunt, 24, 50, 54
Behar, Ruth, 12
Benjamin, Walter, 16
Bhandari, Madan, 42, 44
Bishop, Naomi, 90
Bista, Dor Bahadur, 76
Blim, Michael, 80
Boudhanath (*stupa*), 4–5, 15, 20–2, 26, 37, 46–54, 63–4
Bourdieu, Pierre, 117, 123–5, 141
Buddhism: as ethnic identification, 20–1, 33, 35; as religious practice (*dharma*), 20, 26, 28–9, 84, 87, 132. *See also* Guru Rinpoche, Shakya Lama
Butz, David (with Kathryn Besio), 12

Campbell, Ben, 69
capitalism: global, 8, 24; small-scale (petty), 17, 73, 80
carpet industry, 22–3, 46–7, 51, 52–4, 56–63, 67–74, 76–81, 98, 102; Tibetan weaving tradition, 22, 54, 63
caste (*jati*), 20–1, 31–4, 36, 39, 70, 74, 136
chöten, 84–6, 89, 92–4, 104, 114
Clarke, Graham, 33, 36, 74, 90
class, 44, 69, 73, 136, 140–1
colonialism, 11–12, 23, 47, 49, 127, 144
Comaroff, John and Jean, 24
Communist Party of Nepal (United Marxist Leninists), 31, 42, 44, 91. *See also* Bhandari
Corsaro, William (with Luisa Molinari), 55

Denzin, Norman K., 11
Desjarlais, Robert, 21, 83, 90
Dewey, John, 150–1
discourse, 17–18, 25, 55, 74, 118, 134

economy, 7, 20, 22–3, 46, 59, 61, 62, 70–3, 75–7, 78, 80, 94, 106
education, 133–4
entanglement, 9, 14, 17, 19, 23, 25, 112, 118, 151–2
entrepreneurship, 22, 34, 69–71, 76–7, 80, 89, 113, 151

ethnography, 9–11, 12–15, 18, 75–6, 110, 118, 127–8, 134. *See also* autoethnography

family, 117–8, 123–5, 127–8, 130–1, 134–6
fieldwork, 7–10, 12–15, 17–19, 24–5, 29, 63, 75, 78, 101, 110, 125, 127, 150–1. *See also* autoethnography; ethnography; research ethics
Fisher, James, 45

Geertz, Clifford, 10, 150–1
Gibb, Camilla, 13–14
Giddens, Anthony, 23, 70, 135
gift giving, 82, 83, 85, 110–11, 112, 114, 124, 150–1
globalization, 22, 23–5, 69
Guru Rinpoche (Padmasambhava), 35–6, 62, 81, 87, 95, 103
Guta, Thomas, 62–3

Hastrup, Kirsten, 16
Heider, Karl G., 11
Helambu, 33–6, 38, 44, 69, 74, 84–5, 89–91, 100
Hindu (ethnic and political group), 22, 30, 32–3, 35, 88, 99
Hinduism (belief), 20–1, 33, 35, 86, 132, 144, 147
Holmberg, David, 20
human rights, 7, 18
Hunt, Lynn, 18

Jackson, Michael, 9

Kathmandu (Valley), 7, 19–21, 26, 29–33, 36–7, 40, 42, 47, 49, 97–8, 101, 106, 140, 143–5
kinship, 70, 123–4, 130, 136

Koirala, BP, 34–5, 59, 141
Kondos, Alex, 96–7

labour: child labour, 60–2, 70–1; domestic labour, 106, 121, 123, 124, 130; migrant labour, 21, 97, 100, 101, 126–9. *See also* transnational domestic workers
Luhmann, Niklas, 76–7

Marcus, George, 12
Marx, Karl (with Friedrich Engels), 16
Marxism, 17, 140; neo-Marxism, 73, 80
Milarepa, 27
Misztal, Barbara, 70
Mitchell, Timothy, 49
Montaigne, Michel de, xi
morality, 44, 150–2
Moran, Peter, 28

narrative, 9, 11, 13–15, 18, 36
Nepali (language), 55–6, 58, 82, 132
Nepali Congress, 31, 34–42, 44, 59
Newar (ethnic group), 19, 21, 145

Othering, 10, 12–14, 17–18, 23, 25, 115, 136, 150

Pelias, Ronald J., 13
Prachanda, 141
Pratt, Mary Louise, 9, 11–12, 47

Qvortrup, Jens, 15

Rana family, 21, 30, 32, 34–6, 39, 44, 47–8, 86, 140–1, 144–5; Chandra Shumsher Rana, 30; Jang Bahadur Rana, 32, 141, 144
Rastriya Prajantantra Party (RPP), 21, 31, 34, 39, 96–7

Reed-Danahay, Deborah, 11, 12
religion. *See* Buddhism; Hindu; Hinduism
research ethics, 75, 109–11
Rorty, Richard, 16, 18

Seddon, David, 140–1; with Jaganath Adhikar and Ganesh Gurung, 126
sex trafficking, 121–2, 128
Shakya Lama (Nga Shakya Zangpo) 20, 21, 89, 95, 97–100
Shah dynasty, 31, 35–6, 106, 140–1, 146; Birendra Shah, 34, 93, 106, 140, 144–8; Gyanenda Shah, 108, 148; Prithivi Narayan Shah, 31, 140–1, 144, 147
Sherpa (ethnic group), 19, 33, 49, 52, 65, 85
Shrestha, Nanda R., 94
Stark, Oded, 131
Stoller, Paul, 12, 14

Tamang (ethnic group), 20–2, 24, 33–4, 36, 113
Tedlock, Dennis, 10, 11, 15
Tibetan refugees, 22, 35, 52, 69, 73
Tibeto-Burmese (ethnic group), 20
Tocqueville, Alexis de, 44
tourism, 26, 29, 46, 47, 49, 50, 51–2, 54, 109, 126, 149–50
translation, 11, 16
transnationalism, 17, 24, 70, 100; transnational domestic workers, 106, 117, 121, 126–9, 131; transnational families, 134–5

urbanization, 24, 101
Uttar Bhanjyang, 38, 67, 74, 84–7, 89–91, 97–101, 104, 114

Whelpton, John, 33

Yolmo (ethnic group), 20–2, 24, 33–4, 52, 83, 89

Anthropological Horizons

Editor: Michael Lambek, University of Toronto

Published to date:

The Varieties of Sensory Experience: A Sourcebook in the Anthropology of the Senses / Edited by David Howes (1991)

Arctic Homeland: Kinship, Community, and Development in Northwest Greenland / Mark Nuttall (1992)

Knowledge and Practice in Mayotte: Local Discourses of Islam, Sorcery, and Spirit Possession / Michael Lambek (1993)

Deathly Waters and Hungry Mountains: Agrarian Ritual and Class Formation in an Andean Town / Peter Gose (1994)

Paradise: Class, Commuters, and Ethnicity in Rural Ontario / Stanley R. Barrett (1994)

The Cultural World in Beowulf / John M. Hill (1995)

Making It Their Own: Severn Ojibwe Communicative Practices / Lisa Philips Valentine (1995)

Merchants and Shopkeepers: A Historical Anthropology of an Irish Market Town, 1200–1991 / Philip Gulliver and Marilyn Silverman (1995)

Tournaments of Value: Sociability and Hierarchy in a Yemeni Town / Ann Meneley (1996)

Mal'uocchiu: Ambiguity, Evil Eye, and the Language of Distress / Sam Migliore (1997)

Between History and Histories: The Production of Silences and Commemorations / Edited by Gerald Sider and Gavin Smith (1997)

Eh, Paesan! Being Italian in Toronto / Nicholas DeMaria Harney (1998)

Theorizing the Americanist Tradition / Edited by Lisa Philips Valentine and Regna Darnell (1999)

Colonial 'Reformation' in the Highlands of Central Sulawesi, Indonesia, 1892–1995 / Albert Schrauwers (2000)

The Rock Where We Stand: An Ethnography of Women's Activism in Newfoundland / Glynis George (2000)

Being Alive Well: Health and the Politics of Cree Well-Being / Naomi Adelson (2000)

Irish Travellers: Racism and the Politics of Culture / Jane Helleiner (2001)

Of Property and Propriety: The Role of Gender and Class in Imperialism and Nationalism / Edited by Himani Bannerji, Shahrzad Mojab, and Judith Whitehead (2001)

An Irish Working Class: Explorations in Political Economy and Hegemony, 1800–1950 / Marilyn Silverman (2001)

The Double Twist: From Ethnography to Morphodynamics / Edited by Pierre Maranda (2001)

The House of Difference: Cultural Politics and National Identity in Canada / Eva Mackey (2002)

Writing and Colonialism in Northern Ghana: The Encounter between the LoDagaa and the 'World on Paper,' 1892–1991 / Sean Hawkins (2002)

Guardians of the Transcendent: An Ethnography of a Jain Ascetic Community / Anne Vallely (2002)

The Hot and the Cold: Ills of Humans and Maize in Native Mexico / Jacques M. Chevalier and Andrés Sánchez Bain (2003)

Figured Worlds: Ontological Obstacles in Intercultural Relations / Edited by John Clammer, Sylvie Poirier, and Eric Schwimmer (2004)

Revenge of the Windigo: The Construction of the Mind and Mental Health of North American Aboriginal Peoples / James B. Waldram (2004)

The Cultural Politics of Markets: Economic Liberalization and Social Change in Nepal / Katherine Neilson Rankin (2004)

A World of Relationships: Itineraries, Dreams, and Events in the Australian Western Desert / Sylvie Poirier (2005)

The Politics of the Past in an Argentine Working-Class Neighbourhood / Lindsay DuBois (2005)

Youth and Identity Politics in South Africa, 1990–1994 / Sibusisiwe Nombuso Dlamini (2005)

Maps of Experience: The Anchoring of Land to Story in Secwepemc Discourse / Andie Diane Palmer (2005)

Beyond Bodies: Rain-Making and Sense-Making in Tanzania / Todd Sanders (2008)

We Are Now a Nation: Croats between 'Home' and 'Homeland' / Daphne N. Winland (2008)

Kaleidoscopic Odessa: History and Place in Post-Soviet Ukraine / Tanya Richardson (2008)

Invaders as Ancestors: On the Intercultural Making and Unmaking of Spanish Colonialism in the Andes / Peter Gose (2008)

From Equality to Inequality: Social Change among Newly Sedentary Lanoh Hunter-Gatherer Traders of Peninsular Malaysia / Csilla Dallos (2011)

Rural Nostalgias and Transnational Dreams: Identity and Modernity among Jat Sikhs / Nicola Mooney (2011)

Dimensions of Development: History, Community, and Change in Allpachico, Peru / Susan Vincent (2012)

People of Substance: An Ethnography of Morality in the Colombian Amazon / Carlos David Londoño Sulkin (2012)

'We Are Still Didene': Stories of Hunting and History from Northern British Columbia / Thomas McIlwraith (2012)

Being Māori in the City: Indigenous Everyday Life in Auckland / Natacha Gagné (2013)

The Hakkas of Sarawak: Sacrificial Gifts in Cold War Era Malaysia / Kee Howe Yong (2013)

Remembering Nayeche and the Gray Bull Engiro: African Storytellers of the Karamoja Plateau and the Plains of Turkana / Mustafa Kemal Mirzeler (2014)

In Light of Africa: Globalizing Blackness in Northeast Brazil / Allan Charles Dawson (2014)

The Land of Weddings and Rain: Nation and Modernity in Post-Socialist Lithuania / Gediminas Lankauskas (2015)

Milanese Encounters: Public Space and Vision in Contemporary Urban Italy / Cristina Moretti (2015)

Legacies of Violence: History, Society, and the State in Sardinia / Antonio Sorge (2015)

Looking Back, Moving Forward: Transformation and Ethical Practice in the Ghanaian Church of Pentecost / Girish Daswani (2015)

Why the Porcupine Is Not a Bird: Explorations in the Folk Zoology of an Eastern Indonesian People / Gregory Forth (2016)

The Heart of Helambu: Ethnography and Entanglement in Nepal / Tom O'Neill (2016)